1 —

Flavel
Young

THE SCANDALOUS LIFE OF KING CAROL

OTHER BOOKS BY BARBARA CARTLAND

Novels:

Jigsaw
Sawdust
If the Tree is Saved
For What?
Sweet Punishment
A Virgin in Mayfair
Just Off Piccadilly
But Love Alone
A Beggar Wished
Passionate Attainment
First Class, Lady?
Dangerous Experiment
  (Published in U.S.A. under
  the title "Search for Love")
Desperate Defiance
The Forgotten City
Saga at Forty
But Never Free
Bitter Winds
Broken Barriers
The Gods Forgot
The Black Panther
Stolen Halo
Now Rough—Now Smooth
Open Wings
The Leaping Flame
Yet She Follows

Escape from Passion
The Dark Stream
After the Night
Armour Against Love
Out of Reach
The Hidden Heart
Against the Stream
Again This Rapture
The Dream Within
If We Will
No Heart is Free
A Hazard of Hearts
The Enchanted Moment
A Duel of Hearts
The Knave of Hearts
The Little Pretender
A Ghost in Monte Carlo
Love is an Eagle
Love is the Enemy
Cupid Rides Pillion
Love Me For Ever
Elizabethan Lover
Desire of the Heart
The Enchanted Waltz
The Kiss of the Devil
The Captive Heart
The Coin of Love
Stars in my Heart

Philosophy:
Touch the Stars

Biography:
Ronald Cartland (With a Foreword by Sir Winston Churchill, M.P.)
The Outrageous Queen (The story of Christina of Sweden)
Polly—My Wonderful Mother

Sociology:
You in the Home
The Fascinating Forties

Marriage for Moderns
Be Vivid Be Vital

Non-Fiction:
Bewitching Women

Editor of:
The Common Problem, by Ronald Cartland
  (With a Preface by the Rt. Hon. Earl of Selborne, P.C.)

Radio play:
The Rose and the Violet (music by Mark Lubbock) Performed 1943

Drama:
Blood Money
French Dressing (In collaboration with Bruce Woodhouse)

Autobiography:
The Isthmus Years, 1919–1939
The Years of Opportunity, 1939–1945

Novels signed "Barbara McCorquodale"

Sleeping Swords (Political Novel)
Love is Mine
The Passionate Pilgrim
Blue Heather

Wings on my Heart
The Kiss of Paris
Love Forbidden
The Thief of Love

CAROL II OF RUMANIA

THE SCANDALOUS LIFE

OF KING CAROL

by

BARBARA CARTLAND

FREDERICK MULLER LTD

LONDON

CONTENTS

ILLUSTRATIONS

7

1

1893—1913

A T one o'clock in the morning, Princess Marie of
Rumania lay back on the heavily embroidered
pillows of her bed and watched the aged midwife who her mother-in-law had insisted should supervise
the birth. Methodically the old woman washed the future
heir to the throne, then clothed him in long, heavy
stifling robes.

The Princess had insisted on the curtains of the room
being drawn back. Outside she could see in the October
moonlight the snow on the peaks of the Transylvanian
Alps. Below them the dark beauty of the forests surrounded
the small but lovely palace of Pelishor, older than the
nearby 150-roomed Castel Pelesh, where the King
resided during the hottest weeks of the year.

There had not been much happiness for this vivacious
and beautiful girl, barely eighteen years old, since her
marriage a year before. Her husband, Crown Prince
Ferdinand, was a shy, emotionless man caught up by
circumstances into responsibilities and work for which
he had little talent and less desire.

He had at first been strongly attracted to the girl
selected for him as his wife and future Queen, but totally
incapable of voicing emotion or displaying any passion;
her vivacity and frank delight in the promise of marriage
had appalled and even nauseated him. He took refuge in
a sullen moroseness and strange taciturn shyness which
repressed the groping affection of his young wife, with the
result that the couple were, in reality, strangers to each
other.

A servant had been despatched to Ferdinand's suite to

announce the birth of a son, and the Crown Prince arrived some time later in a dressing-gown. He had been fast asleep despite his wife's long and difficult labour.

"Nando, our son is the living image of you and Uncle," Marie said with eyes that pleaded for a sign of approval. "Shall we call him Ferdinand or Carol?"

Ferdinand, heir to the throne of his uncle Carol I, looked down at the baby held up for him by the midwife. His son's face was almost obscured by the voluminous robes. He felt little emotion beyond a certain relief that he could now hope for a cessation of his uncle's perpetual enquiries about the arrival of the baby and his forebodings that it would not be a boy.

"He must be named Carol," he grunted. "Uncle will insist."

He sensed the need for some gesture or word of affection for the girl whose eyes never left his face.

He cleared his throat.

"You are like a soldier who has just received his baptism of fire," he murmured, and with a formal click of his heels he bent down and brushed his wife's forehead with his lips. His mouth was dry and there was no warmth in the caress. Then, without another glance at the baby, he returned to his bedroom and slept soundly till morning.

Marie laughed weakly as the door closed. Her husband's remark was so typical of the austere and awkward Nando. He controlled his actions and selected his remarks on a basis of a regimental drill book. Every incident in life he dovetailed into a phase of a military manœuvre. She might have known that somehow he would satisfy himself that a woman giving birth to a baby would be symbolic of a soldier's duty. . . .

Drowsiness began to engulf her senses. As she let her relieved body relax into sleep she murmured a prayer, half to herself and half to her God.

"Please let my child be first of all a human being, and

only secondly a Prince. Let him inherit his mother's love of life and all it really means. From my blood let him have the majesty of Royalty and all that he will need to be a King as well as a man. Let not poor Nando's insignificance and timidity mar my baby's life—nor the happiness of the woman he will one day love."

Princess Marie, grand-daughter of Queen Victoria of England and of Alexander II, Tsar of all the Russias, fell asleep. Her God and her hereditary influence had in that minute of time granted her wish: Carol would be no cold and emotionless figurehead. As a new century tossed him and all that he stood for into the whirligig of war, revolution and political upheaval, he would live to become a strange, sometimes pathetic, rarely understood, but always masculine human being. He would be a King with a zest for living.

Carol's infancy was happy and untroubled. His young mother doted on him, and always favoured him more than his sister, Elizabetta, born twelve months after him, or Mignon, Nicolas, and Ileana, born in the years that followed.

His great aunt, the Queen Elizabeth, better known as the eccentric poetess Carmen Sylva, loved the child passionately. To adults, much of her talk consisted of wild ramblings suggesting mental upset. To the little boy who sat at her feet for hours on end, the mixture of Balkan folk lore, classical mythology and the old woman's own interpretations of life were pure romantic delight.

But the pleasant inconsequences of early childhood were doomed to end. The King had indicated year by year his growing dislike of practically everything the vivacious Crown Princess did, not least in the upbringing of her son. Matters came to a head when she accompanied her husband to the French Riviera in the spring of 1897.

Nando had been seriously ill. Doctors recommended convalescence at Nice. The King read the couple a long diatribe about the dangers of life among commoners in a Republic, drew up a list of 'don'ts' and unwillingly let them go.

Marie's activities were reported to Bucharest by toadies of the King. They had little love for the foreign girl who, by sheer force of personality, was drawing to herself a côterie of unimportant but decent people who saw in a woman bred in the traditions of English freedom and democracy an inkling of hope and progress for their own country.

Her most heinous fault, in the eyes of the martinet on the throne, was to attend a masked ball, wearing a dress of black *crêpe-de-chine*, embroidered with gold thread and encrusted with turquoises. Worst of all, she wore scarlet shoes.

The report of her appearance at the ball had instant repercussions. Before she returned to Rumania the King had ordered that he would in future personally supervise the education and care of the Royal children in general and Carol, as prospective heir to the throne, in particular.

Hitherto, Princess Marie had been able to insist on English governesses and nurses having sole charge of her son. Carol spoke English as his natural language, French as a secondary tongue, and Rumanian only as one of his lessons.

Intimidated Rumanian servants replaced the jolly peasant girls Princess Marie had engaged for the menial tasks in the Royal nursery. German spinsters and German pedants arrived to control with the rigid discipline of Potsdam the mental and physical activities of the growing child.

Marie was not a woman to resign herself to the seemingly inevitable. The cunning schemes of the Court to separate her from any position of influence came to nothing, except that they aggravated her emotional estrangement with Ferdinand.

Ostensibly they were still the devoted pair who had received the cheers of the crowds when they drove out from Sigmaringen Castle on their wedding day. In private they merely tolerated one another.

A lesser woman might have taken the easy way of living in luxurious indolence. Marie had such an acute sense of her inheritance and of her destiny that the resistance she met on all sides merely accentuated her resolve to be more than a consort.

Inevitably she attracted the struggling Liberal elements in the country to her side. They saw in her a loophole in the solid wall of reactionary government which surrounded and maintained the throne.

Many of these intriguers got short shrift from the Princess. She had an implicit faith in the divine rights of those of the Royal blood. This—as well as an inborn loyalty to those men she could call her kinsmen—saved her from dabbling too soon in political machinations that would, had they been proved to the King, have finally and completely destroyed her influence.

But there was one man whose character and birth were enhanced by his immaculate reputation. Prince Barbo Stirbey was a scion of one of the most aristocratic families of the Balkans. His quiet and cultured presence had attracted the Queen when she was still a stranger in her adopted land. She liked his retiring personality because of its contrast to the vapid enthusiasm of almost everyone else in the Court, the Government or the Opposition. She also recognised that through him she might in time wield power that would not be attainable by any other means except the corruption and bribery of the real ruling class.

Prince Stirbey, desiring to remain in the background of the political scene, was nevertheless an influential man through marriage. His sister-in-law was the wife of the Prime Minister, and there was no doubt that his advice was sought more often than his brother-in-law, Ion Bratianu, would admit.

In his residence at Buftea, not far from Bucharest,

Prince Stirbey was content to roam among his acres of flowers and to devote his time to his bees. Buftea honey was nationally famous. His deep love for the traditions of his country had also influenced him to start a silkworm farm, in order to revive an age-old industry. He farmed diligently but unprofitably, preferring the charm of cultivated land to a rational business enterprise.

To Bucharest society, whose conversational diet consisted largely of amorous scandal and who had a suspicious distrust of the vigorous and lovely foreigner who was successfully assailing the battlements of the Rumanian-Germanic monopoly of the country, the friendship of the supercilious Prince and the emotional Marie presented a succulent morsel of gossip and innuendo.

There was the time when the carefully tended forest which almost surrounded the Stirbey estates rang with the noise of saws and axes, and tree after tree crashed down, until long avenues broke the serene and leafy skyline which had existed for centuries.

The reason was obvious to the café loiterers of Bucharest. Marie loved riding. She liked nothing better than to drive out of the relaxing heat of summertime Bucharest to the coolness of Buftea, and in the last hour of the day to ride with the Prince.

These expeditions lasted until twilight had turned to darkness. The grooms, attending to the steaming and sweating horses by the oil lamps in the stableyard, noted how hard the animals had been ridden, but no horse, not even Marie's favourite thoroughbred, Grui Sanger, could have been kept at the gallop all the time that she was out.

The Rumanian people of all classes, earthy and for the most part merely a generation or two from a peasant attitude towards life and love, did not hesitate to suggest that the liaison between Barbo and Marie was following a conventional pattern. There was nothing incongruous to them in suggesting that a woman of Royal blood and a man whose entire life was dedicated to upholding the dignity of his ancient family should choose the fields and woods for their illicit love making.

The understanding between the two aristocrats was so close that both must have recognised the indiscretion of continuing their association. But evidently they did not care ; nor did those most directly affected make any marked protest. Princess Stirbey, a physically beautiful woman, was devoted to her daughters and showed what seemed to outsiders to be a genuine admiration for Marie.

There was a room at Buftea where Marie could stay whenever she wished. The Royal children were always welcome, and as a matter of fact they all loved to go there. The rigid masculine manners of the Court would have intimidated any woman, even one blessed with Marie's exuberant character.

At Buftea, cold ritual was softened into a gentle and civilised code of mannered behaviour designed to maintain gracious and pleasant living. And with it there was occasional relaxation of a kind unknown in the Royal palaces.

Carol, ultra-sensitive to his mother's moods, was well aware of her radiant happiness as soon as they arrived at Buftea. He reacted by enjoying himself hugely. The existence of the rather tomboyish Stirbey daughters and of the recreations normal in a country estate meant that at Buftea life could be fun. For a dozen years there was no dark suspicion to mar his joy.

The knowledge of the rumoured scandal came late for a number of reasons. Carol's mother talked in English; the normal language of the Royal family and the courtiers, and even of the politicians, was French. It was characteristic of those whose duty it was to guide and rule Rumania that they considered the native language to be rather vulgar.

Consequently the tittle-tattle of servants, the *sotto voce* gossiping of hangers-on, so fertile a source of news for the normal eavesdropping child, was of little value to Carol. His knowledge of Rumanian was of the schoolbook variety, taught by pedants, and bearing little relation to the colloquial conversation of the lesser people with whom he came in contact during his daily life.

The contemptuous sneer of a German tutor when the boy said something about his admiration for Prince Stirbey may have given him a hint. A growing awareness in early adolescence of the emotional forces which moulded the lives of adult men and women can have started introspective ponderings.

His yearning adoration which was almost a worship for his mother would have done the rest. Prince Stirbey changed from hero to villain in a trice. Carol was jealous of him.

The hot temper which was to send him pell-mell into a thousand ill-conceived acts of bravado rose in his heart until he was choking with anger and tears.

He stormed into his mother's boudoir.

"I demand that you stop seeing Prince Stirbey," he spluttered.

Marie looked at him at first in surprise, and then in horror. Although she knew only too well such gossip existed, she wondered what ruthless enemy she could have who would befoul a child's mind with it.

Then, as her son fell sobbing in her arms, she sighed with relief. Her instinct told her that the boy was making a spontaneous gesture of jealous love for her and that he was not the childish mouthpiece of some vicious courtier.

She calmed him with vague words of comfort and indeterminate denial. The real charge remained unspoken. Neither knew how deeply the seed of dissension had been sown.

Carol's one link of security was almost broken. He was utterly alone. His father he rarely saw, and in any event he did his best to avoid him, for he felt a deep dislike for the way Ferdinand treated Marie as well as a precocious contempt for his status as a puppet.

But most of all, Carol loathed the men who dictated

the fashion of his parents' lives as well as his own. The focus of his dislike was centred on the Bratianu family, the most powerful influence in the country, or, as some said, the only influence. Their attitude to the Rumanian people was worse than feudal because it had none of that patriotic idealism which can use unpleasant means to a glorious end.

As Ion Bratianu left after an audience with Ferdinand, a tittering courtier said within the hearing of the young Prince, " To the Bratianu family, Rumania is not a country; it is a profession!"

Carol never forgot those words.

He writhed in the knowledge that his very existence he owed to the machinations of a Bratianu. He brooded over the knowledge that the self-appointed masters of Rumania had hawked the crown around Europe like a curio, selling it eventually, not for money, but in exchange for a promise of spineless kingship behind whose tawdry façade they could continue to grow more rich and powerful.

Deprived of feminine companionship now that he refused to go to meet the Stirbey girls at Buftea, surrounded by carefully chosen male friends whose eligibility for the Palace was an absence of brains or sensitivity, Carol's formative teenage years passed in deep and desolate unhappiness.

- He kept much to himself, pondering, dreaming, suspecting. He longed to replace his mother on the pedestal where he had first worshipped her. The yearning was unfulfilled.

In January, 1913, Princess Marie gave birth to Mircea, a dark-eyed little waif who was uncannily like her.

Carol, then nearly twenty, adored the baby. The child, fated to die a lingering death from typhoid three years later in the darkest days of the war, caused a profound emotional crisis in Carol's life, bringing with it a psychological injury from which he never recovered.

It was from the innuendos of his companions that he

first heard the suggestion which all Bucharest had known ever since the rumour went around that the 38-year-old Princess was expecting another child. An aspersion was made as regards the paternity of little Mircea.

Carol was accustomed to hide his emotions. He gave no sign that he had heard the over-loud and thickened speech of the half-drunken officer talking to a friend on the other side of the library during a semi-formal reception. But for the rest of the evening he sat brooding and silent, the wine in his glass remaining untouched.

When the party broke up after midnight, he stole along the corridors of the palace towards the Royal children's suite.

An old English nurse started in fright when he opened the door of her room to pass through it into Mircea's night nursery. Her protest was stifled as Carol raised his finger to his mouth, smiled and pointed to the baby's cot. The woman grumbled to herself and lay down. She knew how fond this sad and introspective young man had become of his baby brother.

Carol moved the lamp which burned low beside the cot so that its feeble light fell across Mircea's face. The child was sleeping on his back, the face serene and still.

For fully ten minutes Carol stood there, gazing at every feature, striving to recognise some similarity to the face of the middle-aged Prince he had known so well at Buftea, yet at the same time dreading that he should find a tell-tale characteristic.

There was none. It was also true that he could see nothing of his own father in the child's face. Mircea was ethereal as well as beautiful, different from himself and his brother and sisters despite the pronounced resemblance to his mother which stamped all of the children of Marie.

Carol knelt by the cot in order to look at the child more closely. Not naturally religious, he prayed that night that God would push back the onward march of time and destroy all possibility of doubt about the conception of the baby that slept so quietly; that He would contrive events in the past so that the horrible insinuations against Marie might be refuted and denied beyond all doubt.

Little Mircea stirred when Carol kissed his forehead. The baby's hand, lying on the coverlet, moved in search of something to hold, an instinctive desire for security. Carol put his finger into the tiny hand. The baby gripped him and held on for nearly an hour.

All the time the old nurse had lain awake, wondering what was the reason for this visit. When she saw the haggard misery on Carol's face, her heart went out to the boy—as she still regarded him although he looked a man. He passed by her unseeing, leaving the door open behind him, oblivious of time and place.

By the following evening she knew the reason for Carol's nocturnal visit.

The entire palace staff were agog with rumour. The story a nursemaid brought to the Englishwoman was the most general version.

"His Royal Highness kept to his rooms all the morning," she related gleefully. " He refused to attend luncheon, although some Generals were to be present and a place had been set for him.

"Then about three o'clock he summoned a secretary and asked him to ascertain whether Prince Stirbey was in the palace. He was told that the Prince was at work in the suite Princess Marie had placed at his disposal.

"The Prince put on his uniform as Colonel of his Chasseur Regiment, marched down the corridor and burst into the Prince's room without formality.

"Of course, no one knows what happened inside, but after a few minutes their voices were raised and Corneliu, the young footman who was on duty in the corridor at the time, said he distinctly heard the Prince shout in that high-pitched voice he has when he's in a temper: 'I demand that you never see my mother again.'

"Prince Stirbey's voice was loud and angry too. Corneliu says that he roundly defended himself and denied His Royal Highness the right to meddle in his private affairs.

"Corneliu was nearly caught bending over the keyhole when the door was thrown open and His Royal Highness stalked out. He's always pale, but this time his face was ashen white. Corneliu peeped into the room; Prince Stirbey was standing at his desk shaking with rage and smoothing his cheek with his hand. And Corneliu says"— and the servant girl lowered her voice to a piquant whisper—"that it was plain as can be that Prince Carol must have struck the old chap across the face!"

"Ridiculous!" exclaimed the nurse. "Neither of the gentlemen would demean themselves to bickering like a couple of lackeys. I shall speak to Corneliu and warn him that if he spreads such lies he will find himself out of a job, or maybe in a regiment on the frontier. And you, my girl, had better keep your mouth shut or you will go back to the hovel where you were born."

But nothing could suppress the rumour. Within twenty-four hours it was the *apéritif* at every café table in Bucharest. The Bratianu families and their hangers-on talked it over seriously, scheming to nip in the bud the signs of Royal independence in Carol while at the same time rejoicing in the signs of danger to the power of Marie Mamma.

"Anyway, Germany will soon be at war with the English," a minor relative of the Prime Minister in the Ministry of War told his wife that night. "That will curb the power of this foreign princess. As for Carol, he can fight as an ally of the Kaiser or get out. He will, in any event, learn not to be a nuisance."

2

1913—1916

PRINCESS MARIE learned with annoyance of the stormy scene between her son and Prince Stirbey. But she preferred to remain ignorant of the details, and she did not ask either of the men concerned for his version of the affair.

Carol was too unhappy and desolated to tell her, and Prince Stirbey, with a sense of the appropriate, was careful to steer the conversation from such unpleasant paths when he met the Princess on the following morning for their usual *tête-à-tête*.

Characteristically, the Princess decided that positive action was the best cure for her son's emotional malaise. She was well aware of Carol's affectionate nature and almost neurotic sentimentality. And her common sense deprecated the insistence of her husband and the King that there should be a virtuous cordon of isolation from women around him.

It was obvious that Carol would not be allowed to sow even a handful of wild oats and, accepting the inevitable, Marie busied herself with the possibilities of an arranged marriage which would be politically acceptable to the Rumanian Court.

The personal factors did not worry her at all. Despite her own bitter experience of a marriage of political convenience, she weighed against this disadvantage the likelihood that Carol, as a married man, would gain enough freedom from avuncular and paternal supervision to enable him to go his own way. If the worst happened and his marriage turned out to be only a hollow formality, he could take a mistress. But there was always the chance that his love hunger would idealise the woman he married.

He was good looking, intelligent, witty when the black mood of his depressions was lifted, loyal to a degree, and the type of man who liked to worship a woman.

Marie's thoughts turned first to England. She had a nostalgic love for her own country, and not merely for reasons of family and race.

As she sat in the gold and crimson room of the Palace, where she spent hours in reading newspapers and diplomatic reports, she often wryly pondered on the fact that she might have been the Queen of England.

When she had reached marriageable age there had been many Royal suitors. At sixteen she had been named by newspaper reporters throughout the world as the loveliest princess in Europe.

At that time the Prince of Wales—the future Edward VII—made tentative proposals about the feasibility of a marriage between Marie and his son George. He renewed the enquiries after the death of the Duke of Clarence. Nothing had come of them, first because the relationship was close enough to cast some doubts on the advisability of the union and, secondly, because the intimacy between George and 'Missy' as the Prince called her, was so close that their affection was already that of a brother and sister.

Now, a generation later, a union between the two countries was still unlikely. The eligible girls of England were, in Marie's eyes, unsuitable because as far as she could see, they would bring the future King of Rumania no political advantages. A more valuable connection could be made with the great and friendly power on Rumania's own borders—Imperial Russia.

The time Marie had chosen for these matrimonial negotiations was not particularly promising. The political situation in the Balkans was delicate. In June, 1913, Rumania had declared war on Bulgaria. A comic opera engagement quickly turned to stark tragedy when cholera broke out among the troops, due largely to appalling inefficiency and corruption of the High Commands on both sides.

Rumania gained some territory and a technical victory, but neither the war nor its outcome pleased Russia. The Imperial Government was ultra-sensitive to this irritating Balkan upheaval at a time when they were well aware that a major war was imminent and that their country was completely unprepared.

Consequently, the proposals of the Rumanian Government that a marriage should be discussed between the putative heir to the Rumanian throne and a member of the Tsar's family were not received with great enthusiasm by the Foreign Ministry in Moscow. But the Tsar, anxious to please his beautiful niece, insisted that the idea should be investigated.

The Russian Royal Family was due to take its normal summer holiday in the Crimea, which would be a highly convenient meeting place. After some days sailing around the Black Sea the Russian royal yacht, *Standard*, put in at Constanta, the fashionable Rumanian watering place south of the Danube estuary. There, with a somewhat unimposing entourage which was all that Princess Marie could wheedle out of the Government, Prince Carol was introduced to his prospective father-in-law.

The Tsar Nicolas liked him—and evidently made no secret of the fact, for it was duly noted by Rasputin, who was, inevitably, a member of the yachting party. The monk immediately told the Tsarina that he did not approve of the proposed marriage.

Rasputin's influence over the daughters of the Tsar was secondary only to the baleful power he exerted over their mother. He had, for some time devoted his energies to suggesting that the lovely girls should never marry, but dedicate their lives to some perverted religious mission of his own devising.

Faced with the knowledge that their father might at

any moment force them into marriage, they pleaded with Rasputin for help to avoid such a disastrous end to their plans.

The monk made it his business to meet Carol, and with his uncanny intuitive insight into human character he quickly recognised that the young man longed for love more than for a marriage of political convenience. He learned still more in his brief conversation with Carol.

The Tsar's idea was that an engagement should be arranged with his eldest daughter, the Grand Duchess Olga. Carol had been shown photographs of her. Two of them included her younger sister Tatiana. The Prince admitted to Rasputin that he thought Tatiana was the lovelier of the two.

Rasputin did not underrate the determination of this minor Balkan prince, and he warned both girls that they were in imminent danger of matrimony.

"Prince Carol is undoubtedly of a very affectionate nature. His mouth has a certain lasciviousness about it, and his eyes contain a hint of his regard for feminine pulchritude," he told them. "I am confident that he is so anxious for the joys of marriage that he will go further than his mother or your father in forcing the issue. What I fear is that your own lusts may answer his and swerve you from your dedicated course."

The Russian princesses denied such a possibility in one breath and in the next asked for advice to evade the likelihood of it.

Rasputin's solution was simple.

"Make yourselves as unattractive as possible," he advised. "Coarsen your faces with sun and wind. Dress badly and behave with an ill-bred gaucherie."

The summer of 1914 was a hot one. On one pretext or another, the two girls avoided any meeting with Carol for three days. At the end of it, through exposure to the sun they had ruined their complexions so that they looked like a couple of Ukrainian peasants.

The meeting took place at a dinner on board the *Standard*. Olga had her lower arms swathed in bandages where blisters had turned septic. Tatiana's face was so read and swollen that her eyes were almost closed. Carol did his best to pay court to the younger girl, but long before the meal was over, he had fallen into a sullen silence. The girls had, apparently, no conversation, their table manners were appalling, while their foolish giggling over some secret they shared was embarrassing to everybody.

Only Rasputin was at ease and satisfied.

Princess Marie knew too much about the Rasputin influence not to recognise that it was the monk who was putting obstacles in the way of her plans. She concentrated her blandishments on the Tsar, and almost persuaded him that even if Carol was not interested in Olga there were decided advantages in a union with Tatiana.

But the conversations ended abruptly. Late on the night of June 28th a courier came with the news that the Archduke Francis Ferdinand and his consort had been assassinated in the streets of Sarajevo. The Russian Foreign Ministry appended an appreciation of the situation to this brief report, affirming that war between Austria and Servia was inevitable, with all its eventual consequences to the allies of each belligerent.

The Tsar was many days journey from the capital. Instant orders were given to prepare the yacht for sea. There was a hurried and informal farewell, and Marie knew that her marriage project had failed.

Olga and Tatiana smirked and giggled over their fortuitous escape from a situation that had daily been growing more difficult. Neither could know that, for one of them, the marriage they had spurned would have enabled her to escape the horrors of the revolution.

Carol would have been well content to remain at Constanta for the rest of the summer. The Rumanian skies were as clear and blue as the political skies were dark and menacing. He was fatalistically resigned about the failure of his mother's schemes for his marriage. An element of self-pity was already tending to make him think that he was cursed with a sort of inverted Midas touch so that everything with which he came in contact turned to dross.

There were many attractions to heal whatever slight and ephemeral despair he might have experienced at the abrupt ending to his infatuation for Tatiana. Constanta was full of wealthy Rumanians spending their profits out of the recent war. The freedom from the direct influences of the Court and his mother's tolerance towards his activities enabled him to enjoy an occasional tennis party. He was extremely fond of the game and passably good at it, thanks to the boyhood matches with the Stirbey girls. He could also indulge in his passion for cars.

But the quickening rush to the abyss of general war forced Princess Marie to insist on a return to the Court, which was in summer residence at Sinaia.

Carol showed a petulant annoyance at his mother's haste so that she was both surprised and mystified. He did not tell her that he had heard of the imminent arrival on holiday at Constanta of a girl named Marie-Angele Polizu-Micshuenesti. Wisely, he had told nobody of the silent friendship that had developed between them.

Marie-Angele was an aristocrat but her family was politically of no importance. A series of chance meetings at concerts and at a military review during the war with Bulgaria had insinuated in the minds of both young people that Fate was bringing them together. It was essentially a boy-and-girl romance, with no spoken words of love nor gesture of affection. Their very silence had been expressive of their thoughts and feelings.

Carol prided himself that the friendship was a personal secret. Certainly it was unknown to his mother, but the unseen eyes which watched his every movement had resulted in the inevitable private report to the King. Marie-Angele found that invitations to Royal functions ceased abruptly. Her family was advised of the advantages of a holiday in a distant part of the country while the weather remained so sultry. That Constanta was chosen was a coincidence—but in the eyes of the Prince and the girl it was another proof of the infinite cunning of Fate.

But this time Fate was defeated. Carol was on the way to Sinaia before Marie-Angele arrived. Yet once he got there his existence was almost forgotten while the King, the Crown Prince and the Crown Council met to deliberate on Rumanian policy on the war now bursting with all its fury across Europe.

The date was August 13. King Carol, a Hohenzollern to the core, believed implicitly in a quick and decisive victory for the Central Powers. He went into the conference room determined that before the meeting ended Rumania should have decided to declare her readiness for active military participation in the imminent Teutonic triumph. Ferdinand, who never had definite ideas on anything unless he was told by someone else what they were to be beforehand, agreed to echo the King.

He was, however, worried. Princess Marie, just back from Constanta, had accompanied him to the door of the King's study.

"Don't forget," she said, "that you are first of all a Rumanian and only secondly a Hohenzollern. Remember, too, that England has declared war on Germany, and England always wins the last battle."

He had not answered her, but the impact of her words had tingled in his mind during the three long hours of the Council meeting.

The King found that he could not get his own way. All his advisers were against him except Peter Carp, one of the country's elder statesmen whose love for Germany was exceeded only by his hatred of Russia. The trio of King Carol, Crown Prince Ferdinand and Carp, were quite unable to stir up any feeling of jingoistic patriotism in the rest. The policy was to be neutrality, and it was hinted that if the King did not agree, there was always abdication left as a method of protest.

Carol was with his mother when Ferdinand returned to their suite. Princess Marie wrested the information about the meeting from her taciturn husband in bits and pieces. She heard of the possibility of the King's abdication with mixed feelings. If her husband took his characteristically easy road he would doubtless follow his uncle into exile. If he did this, should she advise her son to proclaim his loyalty and love for Rumania and immediately ascend the throne? And if he did, should she stay with him?

On the other hand, the Bratianu faction, eager to profit from neutrality, might well make the King's abdication the excuse to get rid of the entire Royal family. They would mark time until the war was over, then once again hawk the Rumanian crown around Europe among the Royal families of the victorious powers. The question of Marie's future road was not an easy one to answer.

The three of them drove from the Castel Pelesh, where the conference had taken place, to their own Pelishor residence.

Ferdinand ambled off to his own study, his favourite refuge from the cares of life, where he could read the German newspapers and day dream about the might of Prussia. Marie took her son into the grounds.

There, perhaps for the first and only time in her life, she unburdened her soul to him. She told him of her dreams that he should prove himself a true descendant of Queen Victoria, so that one day he could lead a potentially rich but hitherto mismanaged country into greatness.

"I know the Rumanian people," she said. "I have made

it my business to do so. Their greetings of 'Marie Mamma' are not the sycophantic adulation of the politicians for Royalty, but a genuine devotion. And I will tell you this, they are overwhelmingly in favour of active participation in the war—on the side of Russia, France and England.''

Marie was correct. The mongrel and foreign element which had Rumania by the throat in the commercial and political circles of Bucharest did not reflect the real character of the people. France and Great Britain were nations which the people envied and admired. Russia was by tradition and ties of blood, a friend.

Carol's mind was stirred by the vivid insistence of his mother. The enormity of the immediate future banished the barrier that had come between them since the Stirbey trouble. A new bond of affection and admiration was born that hot summer's afternoon.

Marie left Carol to wander among the woods and fields of the estate. She knew that, whatever the morrow might bring forth, her son's loyalty was, for the time being, to her and not to his father.

Two months later, in circumstances which have never been clearly explained, King Carol I died in his sleep. He had lived long enough to see his invincible Germans and their Austrian allies driven back at the Marne and cut to pieces at Lemberg. It is perhaps reasonable to say that he died of a broken heart. The fact that the country he ruled remained at peace counted but little to him compared with the destruction of a legend of might and power.

For Carol, his new status as Crown Prince and direct heir to the throne brought more privileges than responsibilities. He had more freedom, and he was able to go around Bucharest at night time as much as he pleased.

There were plenty of evenings spent drinking and enjoying the seamier side of one of the gayest cities east of Paris, but the new-found freedom did not go to Carol's head. Some of his cronies complained that he was rather a dull fellow, too interested in the war and in the social revolutions it was bringing.

There were others who felt that this handsome young Prince could be the leader of the action they hoped to take when the old regime was ripe for change. These were middle-aged intellectuals, university students, men who had been educated in Paris, exiles who had grown rich in the United States and had returned through a sense of patriotism when the European war broke out.

Without active work on his part, Carol found himself the focal point of a Prince's party, the members of which were pledged to support him in whatever he did. The fact that the secret police were quite unable to discover any plans hostile to the Bratianu faction or any of the established branches of the Government was a testimonial to the personality of the Prince—a power of which he himself seemed quite unaware. He refused to go in for any subversive intrigue.

Naturally the youthful but potentially influential faction gathered around Carol aroused the hostility of the autocrats around the King. They hinted, quite wrongly, that he was advocating socialism and would lend his name to any move to change the existing order. In fairness to Ferdinand, it may be said that he roundly castigated the statesmen who came to him with this sort of complaint about his son.

Nor did he reprimand Carol for being the cause of such rumours. He filed the information away as merely another example of the strangeness of the children his wife had borne him.

The King's meetings with Carol were irregular. The Palace in Bucharest was used solely for the transaction of State affairs. It was a couple of miles from the centre of the capital, built on the crest of a hill in the midst of a heavily wooded park.

After her husband's accession to the throne, Queen Marie suggested that it would be healthier and more pleasant for the children if their personal residence was in the Cotroceni Palace where they had been living for some years. It was in the big, golden drawing-room of Cotroceni that the decision to declare war on the Central Powers was taken.

It happened on the King's birthday, and seldom can any man have had a more unpleasant gift than what was a virtual ultimatum from his Ministers. Three days later the declaration was handed by the Rumanian Minister in Vienna to the Austrian Foreign Office.

Carol knew nothing of the ultimatum beforehand or the details of its terms. He had seen that Prince Stirbey was once again in close consultation with his mother in the days preceding the declaration of war, and he deliberately avoided meeting them.

He was therefore taken by surprise when the Rumanian and Allied flags appeared in the streets of Bucharest one evening while the crowds swarmed into the streets shouting and singing.

He hurried back to Cotroceni where he found everything in a state of chaos. Fearing air attack, the Royal family was to separate.

His father, who had aged in a matter of hours, tried to display some martial ardour in keeping with his General's uniform.

"My boy, you're now on active service," he said. "You are to accompany me to Scroviste Peris which, for the time being, is the headquarters of the High Command. From now on, of course, you will appear in public only in military uniform."

Carol made no reply. He saw with dislike that his father, despite the tremendous shock of realising he was now the enemy of his idol the Kaiser, was blooming with excitement. This was Ferdinand's opportunity to put into practice all his theories about warfare on the 1870 pattern.

Disconsolately Carol went in search of his mother to bid her farewell. He found her busily supervising the packing of the more valuable pieces of furniture and selecting clothes for herself and the younger children to take away.

"You are leaving here?" he asked.

"Of course," she replied. "It wouldn't be safe. I shall be busy touring the hospitals and I must know that the children are all right when I am not with them. And for myself I must have a harbour in the days to come."

"And the harbour will be where?" he asked quietly.

Marie busied herself with the contents of a drawer in her bureau.

"I shall go to Buftea," she answered.

"Surely there won't be room for everybody?" Carol enquired after a pause.

His mother still kept her face turned away from him.

"The Princess and the girls have kindly agreed to move into that house near the entrance to the estates," she explained. "We shall have the place to ourselves."

"And Prince Stirbey will be on active service, I suppose?"

Marie turned round angrily.

"The Prince has for some time been helping me with my hospital plans," she snapped. "He has been of indescribable assistance. Your father and the Government agree that his organising ability will be best used in continuing that work—at my side."

Carol walked towards the door.

"No doubt he will be adequately supported by Colonel Ballif," he said sarcastically.

He did not notice his mother take a step towards him, her arms outstretched to prevent him leaving. By the time he had closed the door he regretted the cheap gibe about Ballif. It was the first time he had voiced, even to himself, the suspicion that his mother was being indiscreet with her new companion.

Ostensibly the constant presence of the Colonel at Queen Marie's side for the past two years was perfectly rational. The King himself had caused it to be announced that in view of the possibility of war, the Court would be organised on a military basis and that, as part of that procedure, the Queen would have an *aidé-de-camp*.

That Marie had herself selected Colonel Ballif, whose promotion to General after war began was meteoric, not even the War Minister knew. There were times when the King realised that his wife's unconventional activities looked better if he pretended to be the instigator.

Ballif was a competent and reliable cavalry officer whose bearing had impressed the Queen during guard changing duties at the Palace. He was to strangers, austere and unbending, which was, perhaps, as good a method as any of disguising his stupidity. But his dog-like devotion to the Queen more than justified her selection of him as guard, watchdog, and in the years that followed, her general factotum.

By the time war broke out he was the Queen's constant shadow. Carol's reaction to him was largely one of resentment that it was so often impossible to talk privately with his mother. Only after he had taunted her with Ballif by name did he consider any other motive for his dislike. And, as is always the case when a prurient seed is sown in the mind, slanderous innuendo and cruel asides to fertilize his growing suspicions were afterwards constantly to be overheard from fellow-officers.

He saw his mother only occasionally. She had adopted a voluminous costume based on the traditional Rumanian peasant dress. All white, it had a red cross on the tight-fitting cap. Often she rode to headquarters on horseback, giving an appearance, as a cynical British military attaché suggested, of "a modern Florence Nightingale dressed in the costume of an Oriental Joan of Arc."

Despite her ostentation, the Queen was working hard. Her hospitals were better organised than anything else in the gimcrack Rumanian military machine. Carol envied both her efficiency and her happiness in work.

B

In contrast, he had nothing to do beyond inspecting parades of soldiers who were still being trained in peace-time formal exercises and, at the behest of his father, subjected to Prussian ritual discipline.

At the front, the army advanced across Transylvania during the first month without meeting serious resistance. Then the Germans spared a few divisions from France and the painful and inevitable crash to disaster began.

Carol, who had found some tawdry amusements by slipping into Bucharest every evening, heard at the War Council that Constanta had been taken. The news swept his memory back to the hopes he had held when he arrived there only three months before to meet the Tsar and his family.

It seemed like the end of a chapter in his life. With the acute knowledge of an intelligent onlooker he knew that most of the military schemes that were airily outlined at the War Council meetings were both fatuous and futile. He pondered more than his seniors on the black outlook ahead.

3

1916—1918

FOR Carol, the military crisis brought personal relief. He was not without real courage, and he did not fear the rigours of active service. As often as he could he visited the front line.

This kept him away from Headquarters and the sycophantic theorists on strategy who surrounded his father. These encouraged optimism with wild prognostications of what would happen when the Russians sent their promised reinforcements.

For weeks Carol did not see his mother. Then, in the middle of October, while he was on the Northern front, he received an urgent message from her to return to Buftea immediately. Little Mircea was dying.

Thick fog delayed him on the last stage of his journey. He arrived after midnight, and went straight to the room where the child was lying.

The entire family had gathered round the sickbed, including the King. The only light was a holy candle which had been placed on a table beside the bed, with two roses at its base.

Carol, feeling deeply and for that very reason finding himself unable to voice any words of comfort and sympathy to his mother, hung back in the shadows. Near him, erect and silent, and almost concealed by the heavy curtains, was a man in military uniform. Carol thought for a moment it was Prince Stirbey. Then he saw that the figure was that of a much younger man.

He recalled some gossip that he had overheard in a Mess ten days ago when the lights were doused during an air raid. A young Captain had just returned from the

35

capital and was regaling his friends with the latest gossip. "Little Georgie has had a stroke of luck," he said. "As a chap who went through Military College with me and was posted to the same regiment in 1914, I wondered why he hadn't got in touch. Thought he might have been killed—you know how inaccurate the casualty lists are. But he's anything but dead! It seems Marie Mamma liked the look of him, and so Captain Georgescu's name appeared on the Royal Court list for military duty with Her Majesty. Some people strike it lucky! A straight back, a fine pair of moustaches, and there you are! It's a safe little post with quick promotion."

Carol managed to creep out before the 'all clear' permitted the lights to be re-lit. He wanted neither to embarrass the talkative young officer nor to defend a woman for whom he was beginning to feel an angry contempt.

And now, in little Mircea's sickroom, he analysed his feelings for the man standing near him. His mother's lover! He ought to want to kill him. Yet Carol found, a little to his surprise but greatly to his peace of mind, that he felt no hostility whatever towards Captain Georgescu.

The child, Mircea, fought with the uncanny strength of extreme youth against the inexorable forces of virulent typhoid. For nearly a week he lingered on. Carol saw him regularly, but between his visits he avoided the rest of the family.

Mircea died in his mother's arms late one evening almost a week after Carol had arrived at Buftea. The funeral was at the old church of Cotroceni, but the Prince deliberately arrived late and stood at the back.

The funeral arrangements were simple but well arranged. Prince Stirbey had organised everything.

Carol returned to his military duties at the earliest opportunity. His mother insisted on talking to him before he left. Carol never divulged what she had said, while she referred later to her 'tragic conversations' with him without elaborating on them.

A day after Carol departed, Marie and the children were evacuated to Jassy, hitherto a small and sleepy town, but now crammed with Russian troops. There were also innumerable refugees from the invaded areas of the country and from Bucharest itself, which had fallen to the enemy a few hours after the Court and Government had fled.

Carol retreated with his regiment into Moldavia, moving from one town to another as the enemy swept forward. Three weeks of seeing at first hand what war meant hardened him into a man.

When the shattered remnants of the Rumanian forces were re-formed, he found himself once again at Army headquarters and in the company of his father. The Queen came over to luncheon, and afterwards she insisted that she should be told the truth of the military situation.

Carol lounged in the background smoking cigarette after cigarette. He listened poker-faced while Stirbey, Ballif and "little Georgie" discussed the rumour that Germany and Russia had come to a secret understanding about the future dissection of Rumania.

Finally, he made an excuse to take his leave. He was utterly disillusioned about everything and was developing a masocshitic tendency towards extreme pessimism. He expected that he, too, would be destroyed along with the thousands of Rumanians who died daily for a country that had served them ill.

In this introspective, solitary mood Carol discovered that it was pleasant to envisage for himself a hero's death. He found it surprisingly easy to get to the front line. There were influences in the War Council which would not have considered it disastrous if the heir to the throne was effectively removed from the scene by enemy action.

A suicidal gesture to resolve the problem of his life was not, however, to be. In the closing days of the year there was much talk of evacuating the Royal family to Russia. The place chosen was Kherson, an ugly little town east of Odessa, and regarded as safe from invasion.

Carol was brought to Jassy to be told of these plans by his mother. He arrived at the same time as the news that Rasputin had been murdered and that there had been big government changes in Petersburg. Rumour also said that the Empress had emerged unscathed as the most powerful person in the country.

The crisis in the Russian Court after the revelations of Rasputin's diabolism meant that, whatever the military situation, it was not an appropriate moment for the Royal Rumanian exiles to appear on the scene.

Instead Ion Bratianu, head of the newly formed Coalition Government, who had successfully vetoed Queen Marie's own plan for a private diplomatic mission to the Tsar, announced that he would personally try to obtain definite promises of military aid. For reasons of his own, Carol was invited to accompany him.

Queen Marie was well aware that the hostility between her son and herself would now be used as a means to political ends. As Bratianu had intended, his rebuttal of her offer to appeal personally to her kinsman the Tsar was taken as a definite warning that she should refrain from dabbling in military and political matters.

She knew also that Carol was being taken to Russia, not for any aid he could give, but to display to the world the Government's support of anyone who would curb Marie Mamma's influence. To achieve such an end the Bratianu family was ready to lie down with the strangest bedfellows.

To Carol's amazement, he was enthusiastically welcomed in Petersburg by the Tsar, who said that he had by no means forgotten the plans so abruptly cancelled regarding marriage with his eldest daughter.

The Prince was barely civil in his reply. The cynical despair he had felt at the fatuity of his country's war effort was reinforced by the briefest of glimpses of the situation of Rumania's most powerful ally.

The hatred of the people for the Emperor and Empress

was so fierce that it could be sensed in the very atmosphere of St. Petersburg. Worthless men had got into the Government; the few who were honest enough to speak frankly were being banished to Siberia.

Carol requested permission from Ion Bratianu to go home. It was a gesture he hated the more because for the purpose of the trip he had been accredited as a junior diplomat so that Ion Bratianu was his superior, and his Royal status counted for nothing. Permission to return was given.

At Jassy, Carol found his mother agog with excitement about the story that the marriage was again on the *tapis*.

"It will be something pleasant for the people to think about," she said. "I must somehow get to Russia and make definite arrangements."

Carol strode up and down the room.

"There is nothing pleasant about war, and God knows the Rumanian people have been made aware of the fact in the past few weeks," he said slowly. "I don't think that a pretty procession and a peal of wedding bells would delude them. They are too accustomed to processions of ambulances, and to bells that are air raid warnings."

He drew deeply on his cigarette and stubbed it out on the floor.

"In any case there are two good reasons why I think you should reconsider your proposal to go to Russia. The first is that Bratianu will refuse permission. The second is that, while I am resigned to the possibility of being a prince exiled by the declared enemies of my country, I have no intention of marrying an exiled princess who has been driven out by her own people."

"You are talking hysterically," the Queen retorted. "The Tsar is Little Father to his people. They would no more spurn him than deny their God."

Carol shrugged his shoulders.

"We shall see," he said. "My belief is that they will soon do both."

Mother and son met infrequently for the rest of the war. Carol found his own manhood in the crucible of front line action. His new vehemence and obstinacy enabled him again to get away from army Headquarters and take part in the actual fighting. His mother, at first unwillingly and later with pride, recognised that he was as strong-minded as she was. Each respected the other for the ability to get things done.

When Carol found his battle comrades slowly dying in field hospitals where dumps of Russian, French and British supplies rotted unused through red-tape restrictions, he would ask his mother to investigate. Clad in her inevitable white costume, she would descend on the place like a whirlwind. The wounded were nursed, the food supplies were released. Comforts flowed in.

When a French or Russian surgeon sent Marie an exasperated message that he could no longer treat typhus without medicines nor care for the sick without beds and equipment, it was Carol she asked to commandeer what was wanted. He would find what was needed, commandeer transport and press-gang troops and civilians to handle supplies. He never failed her.

The old mutual love was dead, but now there was a new respect to fill the void in the hearts of both mother and son.

The time was not far distant when that respect grew so strong in the mind of the Queen that she was ready to admit the superiority of her son's will power: something that never in the whole of her life did she admit of any other man or woman.

But before that milestone was reached there had been a more serious mental breach between them. In the autumn of 1917, Carol caught jaundice. To convalesce he was sent to Jassy. There he was able with a free conscience to forget the horrors of the front line and amuse himself. By chance he met a charming girl of good family, the daughter of a General.

Zizi Lambrino had, owing to the relaxation of convention in the war and the need to earn money in a town where the cost of even a piece of bread for a civilian mouth reached a fantastic figure, became an entertainer. She performed in one of the few respectable cafés of the town.

Zizi was well aware that the gaunt and yellow-faced young man with the riband of an invalided officer on his arm was the Crown Prince. But she was quite unimpressed. Hundreds of officers had wrongly calculated her price and she had rebuffed them all.

Zizi was a phenomenon in that tawdry wartime town: a completely virtuous girl entertainer. ·

There was in Jassy a circle of young people with the carefree spirit born of disillusion about the present and hopelessness about the future. Gently bred, intelligent, and anxious to remain aloof from the decadence of their elders, they did not drink themselves insensible like some of the wealthy refugees, nor go on repellent carousals like many of the senior elements of the army. They were attractive if rather pathetic in their amusements.

Zizi was among the best known of this circle. Her daring action in entertaining the troops as a paid dancer and singer was envied by the less talented and more timid girls of her acquaintance. Her charm and dark beauty, plus her remarkable talent as a card player, delighted the men.

When she took Carol along to her friends' houses, or to the rooms they had rented—for Jassy was so packed with people that few indeed had an entire house to themselves—they automatically accepted him as one of themselves. With Zizi as a sponsor he became *persona grata* without question or excitement in a social circle he could hardly believe existed.

For the lonely Prince, so accustomed to be treated with the deference due to his rank or else with scarce-concealed contempt by the politically powerful families of Bucharest, life became sheer joy. It was not long before he had fallen deeply in love, and in the delightfully unrepressed environment in which he found himself he made no attempt to conceal the fact from his new friends.

It was some time before he told Zizi. She accepted it without surprise.

"I know you love me," she said with unaccustomed gentleness. "Everybody has been telling me for days past that I've hooked a Prince! I haven't told them that I'm more fond of you than I would have thought possible."

"I am going to marry you," Carol said bluntly.

Zizi took his arm and smiled up at him.

"Let us go for a walk," she suggested. "I want to get away from everybody where we can talk. We have got to be sensible about this. I'm a commoner. You are the Crown Prince. Marriage is impossible!"

They walked in silence until they were on the outskirts of the town. There were vineyards on either side of the road, the vines neglected and broken. The frost in the air made Zizi shiver, and Carol put his arm round her.

"Tell me that you love me," he pleaded.

"You ought to know by now that if I love a man it doesn't matter who he is," Zizi said quietly. "Love is something no one can help—or stop."

His arm tightened and he drew her closer.

"You must be my wife," he said. "I want you to belong to me—to be all mine."

He began to kiss her and they clung together, a flame of passion consuming them both. After a while Zizi whispered: "And I want to belong to you—but there is the war and who knows what chance there is of us remaining alive. Love is all that matters—love like ours."

They turned and walked back to the town. Carol took Zizi to the café where she was supposed to entertain the patrons. It was already past the usual time of her performance.

She drew him past the door. "I'm not going there to-night," she said. "And perhaps never again."

He nodded and walked on with her. Zizi had a room in the house of a distant cousin. The house was an old one, with many large rooms. In every one of them beds had been erected. Children, babies, men and women of all ages were crammed together in a colony of relatives.

No one worried about the entry of two young people who tip-toed up the stairs in the darkness. No one would have recognised them if they had been seen because the black-out was strictly enforced by patrolling troops who doused with a rifle bullet any light they saw.

Carol made no secret of his love affair. He was with Zizi every moment of the day. He took her to luncheon and dinner at the hospital mess. He introduced her to officers of high rank and brought her along to receptions given in aid of the Red Cross by aristocratic and wealthy hostesses. In a matter of days all Rumania knew that the Crown Prince was infatuated with a beautiful commoner.

Emissaries came hot-foot to Jassy at the behest of both the King and Queen who had left the town for work in other areas. They passed on messages from Ferdinand recording his extreme displeasure. Carol walked out of the room while they were still mumbling the threats they had been told to make.

The Queen's representative followed more subtle methods. They moved heaven and earth to uncover some scandal about Zizi's life. They had to report to Marie that the girl's virtue was a byword among her friends and the subject of jokes about the impossibility of anyone assailing her purity.

The battle grew more bitter. The King ordered the doctors to examine Carol and to report that he was again fit for duty. This was not difficult for by December he had completely recovered from his attack of jaundice.

The continuing deterioration of the war situation brought the army chiefs to Jassy for a final stand. Arrangements were also made for the flight of the Government and Court into Russia if the worst happened.

Carol did not underrate the venom of his enemies. He drove Zizi by car to a remote village closer to the border where, if it was necessary, she could escape to safety and would in any event be able to live for the time being in secrecy and security.

This was a wise move. The King, who could never make up his mind about military matters, bestirred himself to devise plans to kidnap Zizi and throw her into prison. He was frantic with anxiety to prevent his son besmirching the Royal line which, from the dim past of petty European monarchy, had through a long succession of loveless unions hitherto been kept pure.

Queen Marie, only too acutely aware of the forceful impetus of love, knew that brash and brutal actions of this kind would merely further antagonise Carol and engender all his latent powers of resistance. She decided that to defeat him she must use cunning.

She arranged for him to be overwhelmed with military duties. He was sent hither and thither on courier work which could have well been carried out by a dispatch rider or by a junior adjutant.

The growing number of Carol's allies in this romantic impasse said with some justification that these military errands often tended to take the Crown Prince into areas where casualties were high. It was no fault of the High Command that the casualty lists did not include a Royal name on at least a dozen occasions.

Carol parried all efforts to break his will by these methods. He went off willingly and conscientiously, carrying out his orders almost to the letter. Only sometimes the route he took was not the prescribed one. By driving fast in his Rolls Royce he outran any prying pursuers and managed to spend a few enticing hours with Zizi in her hideaway.

Marie had no proof that Carol was doing this, but by the simple process of putting herself in her son's place she realised that he was probably seeing his beloved regularly.

At a stormy meeting with her husband she insisted that the military missions should end and that Carol should be kept under surveillance in Jassy.

She got her way, and Carol became her chauffeur, driving his mother and Ballif on tours of canteens, hospitals and refugee centres. He acted like an automaton. He sat woodenly at the wheel of the car, walked stiffly behind Marie and Ballif when they inspected hospital wards.

The clashing temperaments of mother and son were irresistible forces meeting head on because they were evenly matched. Both knew it, and if it had not been for the fantastic seriousness of the situation which made every day one of horrifying unreality, one or other would have given way. But they were both obstinate to the point of absurdity.

The Bolshevik revolution and the ensuing Russo-German armistice, the complete chaos in the Ukraine and the fomenting of revolution in the Rumanian areas where Russian troops were stationed all brought nearer and nearer an imminent doom to life and love alike.

In January, 1918, the Bratianu Government threw in its hand after Germany sent an ultimatum insisting on peace conversations. But the King and his generals obstinately insisted on a melodramatic rejection of the offer. A particularly wooden-headed martinet, General Averescu, formed a government which promised to prove that the position was neither hopeless nor tragic.

Within three weeks the General had to bow to the inevitable. The Crown Council was summoned to agree to the enemy's terms.

As usual in times of deep crisis which was not of their making, Marie and Carol forgot their differences and were drawn close together. The Queen still had implicit faith in the Allies' power to win, and she was ready to go to any lengths to ensure that Rumania remained in the war. On the morning that the Council was due to meet she begged Carol to come to her room and have breakfast with her. For an hour she explained the situation to him.

The King came in, and noting how abruptly conversation had ceased, suspiciously demanded to know what they had been talking about. He spoke only to the Queen. Mentally at least he had long before disinherited Carol.

"Carol has to attend the Council this morning," Marie replied. "He wishes to know what has been happening, and I have explained the situation to him."

"That is unnecessary. His duty is to support me," the King replied coldly. "And there is no need for you to dabble in affairs which only concern the State."

His words aroused the Queen's passionate anger. She lost her temper and poured out a flood of bitter truths which at first left the King speechless and later aroused his protests. Carol infuriated him still further by repeating with absolute calmness all that his mother had voiced in a fury bordering on hysteria.

The quarrel had one beneficial result. The King had intended to confirm without question the proposed acceptance of the peace terms. As a result of Marie's frenzied efforts to arouse his self-respect he begged his ministers to think things over and meet on the morrow.

When the Council met the following day, Carol did not sit down at the conference table but wandered around, smoking, and staring out of the windows. No one troubled to speak to him. But now he spoke every member turned in surprise at the firmness of his voice as he echoed the King's plea for further deliberation.

This was the one source of encouragement, the only support for the King. Once again the troublesome worry of this determined young man aggravated the thoughts of the politicians.

On the next day they had further proof of his personal views. Ferdinand refused to see his wife in the intervening period. But Marie got hold of Carol at breakfast and begged him to make one final gesture of defiance.

"In the middle of the conference," she said, "when it is obvious that your father is about to give way, stand up and protest in my name, and in the name of all the women of Rumania, against this horrible peace."

Carol listened, but voiced no actual promise that he would do what she asked.

At the meeting the King muttered in a voice that could hardly be heard that as he was unable to organise a united Government to carry on the defence of the country he was ready to accept the enemy's terms.

His capitulation had been a foregone conclusion, and the members began to collect their papers preparatory to leaving.

Carol stood up, and in the rather high-pitched voice he had when excited, repeated his mother's words.

No one took the slightest notice.

He half ran from the room. By the time he reached the Queen's apartment he was crying. He fell into her arms. She held his head against her breast, stroking his hair as she had not done for a dozen years. It was the last time that they expressed their love for one another in visible form.

Later that day the King vehemently complained about his son's melodramatic behaviour.

The Queen smiled sweetly.

"The boy meant well," she said. "Carol never doubts that he is right and is entirely justified in all he does."

"That is exactly what I am complaining about," muttered the King.

The virtual disintegration of the country with the cessation of hostilities loosened the bonds which prevented Carol from seeing Zizi. Throughout the spring and summer of 1918 he was constantly in her company, although he was still careful to be discreet about it.

His love for her grew with every moment of intimacy. Cynical and disillusioned by the fate of royalty all around him, he lost whatever few misgivings he might have once felt about marriage with a commoner.

Carol met many young officers of the Russian army who had decided to go over to the Bolsheviks; he began to understand their reasons. The vile treatment of the Tsar and his family did not entirely abolish the suspicion that it was their own behaviour which had made such bestiality possible.

Carol had also seen the divine right of kings destroyed in an hour with the abdication of King Constantine of Greece the previous autumn. He knew that King Ferdinand of Bulgaria would be the next to go, and he suspected that there might be no throne for him to ascend in Rumania.

He felt no compunction in organising his private life as he wished, irrespective of the duty that had been pummelled into him from infancy.

In August, 1918, he made his plans—at first against the wishes of the devoted but fearful Zizi, but later, when she wonderingly accepted his unswerving decision, with devotion and quiet encouragement.

Carol made up his mind to marry her with all the panoply of religion so that there could be no question of the legality of the union.

A wedding ceremony in Rumania was out of the question. No priest would have dared to conduct the service except as a secretive affair, which was the last thing Carol wanted.

With the help of several young officers of the demobilising Russian forces and of his own Rumanian regiment he smuggled Zizi across the frontier and reached Odessa.

Communication facilities of an official nature between Russia and Rumania were non-existent. Private messages took days to get from one country to the other. Carol was able to arrange a wedding ceremony without any information about it reaching Rumania.

He was not religious—a factor not unexpected in view of the divergent beliefs in his family. King Ferdinand was a devout Roman Catholic, despite the penalties of his

Church which withheld her consolations from him when
he agreed, on ascending the throne, to allow his children
to be brought up in the Greek Orthodox Church. Queen
Marie was a Protestant. As a result, Carol's spiritual life
was as bewildering a mixture as every other aspect of his
education.

Yet he desired above everything that his marriage with
Zizi should receive the full blessing of the Church—a
factor which he knew would count greatly with the
Rumanian people.

The ceremony was held in the Cathedral Church of the
Intercession of the Virgin at Odessa. The rites were
administered by the greatest church dignitaries that
could be mustered in the Southern Ukraine. Immediately afterwards the bridal pair started for home, travelling
openly and triumphantly together.

Carol could not have estimated the furore which his
marriage would cause. By the time he reached Jassy, his
friends were able to tell him that his life was in danger.
The Bratianu faction were busily persuading the King
to have his son shot as a traitor.

The Court was back in Bucharest. The Queen recorded
in her diary that the news of the marriage was "an almost
insurmountable grief, a staggering family tragedy which
hit us suddenly a stunning blow for which we were entirely
unprepared. I have had many difficult battles to wage,
but this was the most terrible of all, because it meant we
had to fight against one of our own, to save him against
his own will."

Carol had no desire to be saved. It was not the
emotional fever of a love-sick bridegroom that influenced
him to write to his father and inform him that he intended
to renounce his rights to the throne. He did so because he
felt no sense of mission in kingship, with or without the
woman he loved.

Ferdinand, on receiving this brief message, was so
furious that he instantly made more definite moves to

combat the situation than he had ever done against his political and foreign enemies.

He telegraphed to a Colonel on his staff who was still at Jassy:

"You are ordered to escort the Crown Prince to Bucharest immediately. Before being authorised to use force you must make sure that there is no hope of inducing the Prince to return to a sense of realities. If the Prince is irrevocably decided, you are to point out to him in his own interests the serious effect which a final rupture with his family and his country would have."

Zizi persuaded her husband to go to Bicaz, one of the Royal residences in the country, where the Court had gone for peace and quiet, and talk with his parents. They refused to see him. Carol retaliated by sending for his wife and again applying formally for an interview with his father. The King thereupon issued an order that his son should be arrested.

As Commander-in-Chief of the army and Carol's superior officer the King held a highly unconstitutional court martial without the prisoner. He then issued a verdict of treasonable conduct with a sentence of seventy-five days' close confinement on a bread and water diet in the military prison of Bistrita. Fortunately his officers had the sense to ignore the order and Carol remained free.

When Queen Marie, genuinely distraught and indignant, finally met her son, she burst into tears. Carol remained unmoved and returned as quickly as possible to Zizi in the small house outside Bucharest, for which she paid the rent. The Crown Prince of Rumania was to all intents and purposes, penniless.

Greatly interested in the outcome of the scandal was the ex-Prime Minister, Ion Bratianu. He visited Carol, bearing a false and artificial olive branch of friendly understanding. His aim was to discover whether the Prince wished to renounce the throne because of his unwillingness to rule, or because of his insistence that his wife should be accepted as a royal consort.

Having seen Carol he spread the news that the Prince
was ready for his marriage to be annulled.

No one believed that Bratianu's report of the conversation was accurate. But it was generally accepted that the
best way out of future trouble was to find some loophole
in the legality of the wedding ceremony, announce it to
the people with an air of patriotism, and leave the next
move to Carol.

Advisers persuaded the King and Queen to desist
from their melodramatic denunciation of their son, and
for the edification of the public to make some show of
family serenity.

Financial allowances were restored to the Crown
Prince. He was invited to take part in the celebrations of
the Allied victory, and on November 18 he rode through
the streets of Bucharest at the head of his regiment. He
was, however, kept well away from the rest of the Royal
family.

The King, Queen and Prince Nicolas rode at the head
of the procession on horseback; the children came close
behind in carriages. Carol's detachment was half a mile
to the rear. It was noted with many misgivings by the
assembled ministers that the crowd's cheers for Prince
Carol were tumultuous, often far louder than for the King
himself.

Carol took no part in the ensuing religious service of
thanksgiving in the Metropolitan Church, nor in the State
Banquet that evening. He had gone straight back to Zizi.

"To-morrow they will order their jurists to start
proving my marriage illegal," he told her that night
while they tossed sleepless in bed.

"And suppose they succeed?" Zizi whispered.

"They can't, it is impossible," Carol positively insisted.
"We are married in the sight of God and man, and
nothing that God or man can do will alter the fact."

"Anyway, we will still have each other," Zizi murmured. "Oh, darling, I love you so much."

The legal joke was played out with full ceremony.

The Rumanian Supreme Court listened for days to arguments to prove that no member of the Rumanian Royal House could marry without permission of King and Government. The interminable lawyers' monologues trapped out the whole sorry business with some sort of superficial legality.

There was nothing more than a formal objection in favour of Carol, and that just for the sake of appearance. The foregone conclusion was confirmed in the solemn words of the High Court Tribunal. The marriage of Crown Prince Carol and Zizi Lambrino was "unconstitutional and illegal", and it was formally pronounced "null and void".

Carol's answer was two-fold. Publicly he repeated his determination to renounce the throne. Privately he told Zizi: "Whatever the Tribunal says, I shall never cease to regard myself as your husband."

Zizi, now pregnant, believed him. She loved him to the exclusion of all else—even fear of the future.

4

1919

POLITICALLY the situation had reached a stalemate. Carol continued to live with Zizi.

The Government, reading the reports of the secret police sent from every town in the country, had to admit the fact that the Crown Prince was exceedingly popular. An official acceptance of his offer to abdicate would, the police reported, arouse civil disturbances. The press had soft-pedalled his "irrevocable decision" to do so into a euphemistic "proposal".

Carol had good friends in the police circles, and the fact that the Court had no trump for his ace was duly reported to him.

He frankly did not care one way or the other. His devotion to Zizi was so intense that an hour in her company banished every qualm about a future where he would be an impecunious private citizen in exile. He was never very far from her comforting arms so that his doubts were rare and short-lived.

But he underrated his adversaries. While the King muttered about incarceration in monasteries where lascivious desires could be purged by the cleansing discipline of harsh religious exercises, the Queen had more potent plans.

She understood only too well her son's amorous nature. She correctly assessed that the physical side of his love was of paramount importance to him.

He also worshipped beauty as much as he loathed ugliness. From a small child he had remarkable good taste. The vulgar ostentation of many of the Rumanian homes of the political upstarts disgusted him even as a mere boy just as the priceless treasures in his father's palace entranced him.

Beautiful women, considered the Queen, would inevitably attract and enthrall her son. Despite his wish to love only Zizi he would willy-nilly look on other loveliness with yearning and, eventually, desire.

A hint to the Government was all that was necessary. Court officials, deeply worried about the health of the country only slowly convalescing from the almost mortal malady of war, hurriedly organised the machinery of seduction. They ranged far and wide for the bait which was to entice the Crown Prince from his pledge of marital fidelity.

Prostitutes, with the aid of a lavish official grant, found themselves out of the Bucharest brothels and off on a spending spree in the best shops of the city. The mistress of one of the General Staff, the toast of half a dozen regimental messes, was dazzled with the hint of a still more notable lover if she would exert her charms when and where she was told.

Wives and daughters of families high in Rumanian society, whose moral laxity was well known, got the briefing for an exciting new romance. Italians, Frenchwomen, and one white Russian Duchess arrived in Bucharest to enter the competition. London lost a notable specimen of the first generation of the new Bright Young Things.

For some time Carol withstood the blandishments of these hirelings. He was at first flattered at the number and variety of invitations which were sent to him. He was pleased when they included his wife, despite the legal theory that she was now merely his mistress.

It took him some time to notice the snubs that Zizi received. He was drinking heavily at this ceaseless round of parties, so that his sensitivity was numbed.

Zizi became unwell. She suffered from morning sickness and the nausea was aggravated by their late nights. As the weeks of pregnancy advanced it became impossible for her to accompany her husband to any but the smallest and most informal functions.

Carol, for all his bravado that Zizi was still his wife, was not pleased about the coming child. He saw all too clearly that even if conception before the annulment could be proved, the baby's legitimacy would be the subject of prolonged legal wrangles. And he was already feeling the pangs of paternal jealousy. He wanted Zizi all to himself.

If these thoughts were the fundamental cause of his growing restlessness, a more insistent motive was Zizi's fading beauty. Pregnancy makes some women glow with a loveliness that is almost supernatural. Zizi was not one of them. The nausea, the size of the embryo child, and her lassitude made her ugly, and no amount of sentimentality about her womanly rôle could minimise the fact.

She dreaded the birth, with the illogical panic of a woman who is convinced that she will die in labour. Her fear turned the once gay and vital girl into a weak, whimpering woman, full of forebodings, pleading for comfort, begging for sympathy.

Her health was so bad at this time that, utterly miserable because she still loved Carol with a fiery passion, she had to tell him their physical relationship must cease. Carol was extremely virile, exacting and selfish in his sexual appetites. There were stormy scenes, bitter words —and usually the end to them was that Carol stalked out of the house.

He was ripe for infidelity, but it is true to say that he was seduced from his wife rather than that he deliberately betrayed her. Every time it happened he was ashamed and came home to Zizi, repentant and unusually kind and gentle.

Instinctively she guessed the motive for his abrupt changes of temperament. And she would weep bitterly, the tears rolling down her haggard face and her swollen body shuddering as his hands tried flatteringly to caress and reassure her.

Not once did she directly charge him with infidelity; not once did he confess it. The very silence made both accept that the other knew. The hurt for both was terrible.

Carol took to sleeping away from home, sometimes at the Cotroceni Palace, sometimes in the apartments of his mistresses. The nights became week-ends and, in the autumn, week-long holidays in the country. His marriage with Zizi just withered away.

Zizi gave birth to her child on January 20th, 1920. Carol had made no enquiries about her for nearly a month. He had sent a Christmas gift with a formal note of good wishes. He had not thanked her for the framed photograph of herself taken when she was the gay young girl of war-time Jassy. It was all she could afford to send and all that she wished to give him—a reminder of past happiness and an embittered comment on her present misery.

Mutual friends told Carol that he was father of a fine boy. He sent some flowers and with them a note saying: "Please call him Mircea."

Zizi kept that note for the rest of her life. She, who had listened to the secret agonies of Carol's soul knew that he had chosen the name in memory of his little brother. He had never forgotten the night when he had sat beside the dying infant, holding the weak little fingers in his, and praying that his suspicions of the child's paternity should prove groundless.

Although Zizi's pregnancy had long been known to the Court, the actual birth accentuated the urgency to do something definite to destroy the "liaison", as it was now called.

The facts were that, despite the legal triumph in the Rumanian courts, the victory was a hollow one. Thrones had consistently toppled since 1914, and the world's press was alive to the possibility of a story of a new Royal downfall. In any event a Royal romance was just the story a war-jaded world needed.

A discreet glossing over of the facts of history enabled journalists to describe Rumania as "a gallant little ally", who had fought against impossible odds in the Balkans on behalf of her big sisters in the West. Carol was a warrior prince whose war-time experience had given him a democratic outlook so that he had revolted against the outmoded protocols of royalty and sought love instead of power.

No musical comedy about Ruritania could vie with the real-life, romantic story of Rumania. No Prince Charming was so handsome, so gallant, so reckless of turgid advice as Prince Carol. Cinderella was personified in the glamorous Zizi.

Every act in the romantic drama was a box-office hit. The accidental meeting; the elopement to Odessa; the heavy father and the heartbroken mother; the cruel imposition of the law, the wicked temptresses, the first cry of the little one. The recipe was complete. Fleet Street and Times Square only regretted that Grandfather Ferdinand had not thrown mother and baby into the snow-covered streets of Bucharest on the January morning when his grandson was born.

Queen Marie, an avid reader of cosmopolitan news-papers, knew all about the glamour that surrounded her son's romance. As a woman she almost rejoiced in it. As a Queen she recognised it was disastrous to her high ambitions for him.

Her decision to call the world's bluff was the right one, but it took her a long time to convince her husband and his ministers of its efficacy. Instead of concealing the Prince in garrison towns, monasteries or prisons, instead of standing on the pompous dignity of a minor Balkan monarchy, she advocated that Carol should be put on display.

"Send him round the world," she told Ferdinand.

"Get the Government to grant him a lavish allowance. It will do Rumania good, for there is nothing that all these new republics and people's democracies will love so much as a Crown Prince."

She smiled, then added:

"They will also see another side of our son which the press doesn't report. I am afraid that, emotionally, Carol is not the immaculate knight in white armour that foreigners have been led to imagine."

The King glowered at her.

"I fail to see how rewarding him with a holiday is a just punishment for the harm he has done to our name. Besides," he added, "if he's not in Bucharest we can't control his activities. He'll probably take that woman with him."

Queen Marie shook her head.

"I come from a country with a large number of colonies," she replied. "It is a tradition of England that men whose hearts are broken, or those who are crossed in love, must go abroad to forget. Believe me, it always works."

The King remained unconvinced. But the Bratianu faction, whose motto was to do everything by stealth and who implicitly believed that the most effective actions were those which seemed to be anything but what they really were, soon came round to the Queen's point of view.

Carol was duly told that he was to travel as a roving ambassador for his country. Regrettably, the duty of imparting this information was left to the King, who did his best to make it sound like a penance. Carol, truculent and angry, listened to the harangue which might have been given to a naughty schoolboy.

The King had summoned him during the normal morning audience, thereby making the conversation both formal and official. That afternoon, Carol ordered his horse to be saddled, and told the grooms that he was going for a gallop. He refused to allow an equerry to accompany him. He was in military dress, and carried a revolver in his saddle holster.

Two hours later the horse trotted into the stableyard. Carol was slumped in the saddle. His tunic was bespattered with blood, and one of his black riding boots was stained crimson.

The alarmed groom summoned help and the Prince was gently lifted down from the horse. He was carried into the saddle-room and laid on some straw while a doctor was summoned. Queen Marie arrived just as the doctor had completed his examination.

"A superficial wound, fortunately, your Majesty," he told her. "Or rather, two superficial wounds. There is no danger to His Royal Highness's health or life. But he will, of course, have to rest for a time."

The man hesitated and looked uneasy.

"Perhaps your Majesty would like me to wait until you have seen the Prince."

The Queen hurried indoors. Her talk with Carol was brief and one-sided. He muttered that he had had an accident while drawing his gun to fire at some wood-pigeons.

"With a revolver?" she demanded. "And you suffered two accidents with two consecutive shots?"

Carol closed his eyes and would say nothing more.

Deeply worried, because she had never envisaged a suicidal trait in her son, the Queen gave orders for the Prince to be removed to the Palace where she could nurse him personally. When that was done, she ordered the doctor to stroll up and down the yard with her, out of earshot of the stable hands.

"I think I remember you, Doctor, at my field hospital at Tecuci?" she began.

"Yes, your Majesty," the doctor answered with pride. "You congratulated me on a leg amputation I was just completing. Your Majesty was an inspiration to us in those terrible days."

The Queen was relieved to know that she had found a staunch ally.

"For the sake of those times," she said, "I rely on your absolute discretion in this present matter. I would remind you of your Hippocratic oath and beg you, as a mother—rather than order it as your Queen—that you refer to this as an accident."

"It was, as your Majesty says, an accident," the doctor replied.

It was perhaps fortunate that the injuries, having been deliberately inflicted, were slight. One bullet had merely nicked the fleshy part of the heel; the second had burned and torn the left shoulder near the neck. Carol had lost a considerable amount of blood from the latter wound, where the metal badge on the collar had deflected the bullet slightly so that it had gone deeper than he had intended.

But neither the gesture of protest nor his injuries brought any change in the King's decision that Carol should go on the world tour. It delayed matters a few weeks, by which time the Prince was himself becoming keen on the idea. He was suffering increasingly from bouts of enthusiasm and depression. He wanted badly to get away from the rows and intrigues.

One twinge of conscience needed to be assuaged. He asked his mother outright what would be done for Zizi and her child.

"On the day that you agree to an announcement in the Court Circular giving details of your itinerary, she will be handed a draft for £10,000 sterling."

"And the catch in it?" Carol asked cynically.

"The catch, as you call it, is merely that she will agree to live in Paris for the rest of her life."

"She won't take it, you know," Carol pointed out, with an almost boyish grin of nostalgic admiration that cut Marie to the heart. "You ought to know by now that Zizi is very proud."

"I think she will accept the money," his mother answered. " You have not been able to be exactly generous to her recently. For herself I agree this might not matter. But she has a child. It may not be true that every woman has her price, but no mother will allow her child to suffer unnecessarily."

"If you can bring me a truthful report that Zizi is agreeable, you may have the Court announcement drawn up," Carol answered.

Zizi took some convincing. It was a week before an aunt of hers arrived at the palace and quietly told Carol that his wife was grateful for the generous arrangement that had been planned.

"I propose taking Mircea and her to Paris the moment we can arrange the journey," she added.

Carol's world tour was announced. Barely a month was allowed for the preparations. While the Court officials organised diplomatic matters, Carol went to bid farewell to the officers of his Chasseur regiment stationed at Bistrita in the North of the country.

He had gone to the garrison town on frequent occasions since the deterioration of his intimacy with Zizi, usually to escape some pretentious Court affair or to evade an incipient argument with his mother.

He liked army life, and he liked Bistrita in particular. The regiment had settled down to peace-time routine. It was to be stationed in the area for years to come, and most of the married officers had bought houses in the town.

Far from the conventions and intrigues of Bucharest, this little military colony in the foothills of the Carpathians provided good hunting, good company, and an easy, untrammelled existence.

Carol's great friend, a war-time comrade-in-arms, Captain Tempeanu, had been given a commission during the hostilities almost solely on his abilities. He had signed on in the re-constituted Rumanian army after the

Armistice. He was a quiet, pleasant man, serious about his career, but with a charm and unaffectedness that had immediately attracted Carol.

He had married a beautiful red-haired girl, vivacious and intelligent. She was well-known for her hospitality and her ability to cook traditional Rumanian dishes.

Naturally, Captain Tempeanu invited his Commanding Officer to his home. Carol went once as was his duty. After that he went time and time again on account of the quiet charm of the house and the sympathetic friendliness of his hostess.

Now, as the months of absence loomed ahead, he felt that he must return once more to say good-bye. The Tempeanus made him welcome. Elenutza cooked a splendid meal and talked animatedly of the wonders Carol would see on his tour. Afterwards the trio played cards till early morning.

Elenutza always impressed the male guests in her home with her flair for cards. She was a rarity among women, a player who never betrayed by a tremor of her hand or a sign on her face whether things were going well or ill for her. As a poker player she was famous among the officers, and for the same reason, heartily disliked by their wives.

It was said, not without some justification, that the generous hospitality at her house, which would have been impossible on Captain Tempeanu's pay and modest private resources, was due to her gambling victories. Many a guest paid handsomely for his dinner by the painless extraction of money at cards. On the other hand, quite a number of penniless young lieutenants went away richer when their hostess appeared to have a run of bad luck.

Elenutza was a clever and calculating woman, determined that her husband should move fast along the road to success.

Watching the cards with wide-awake, grey-green eyes

in a face as smooth as fine porcelain, she never appeared
to be the ruthless player dependent on winning. Equally,
she never embarrassed those she had decided to help by
a display of gaucherie.

Other officers' wives in the garrison snubbed Carol or
fawned on him, according to their views regarding the
Crown Prince's future. Elenutza Tempeanu treated him
as a man she liked, and no more.

It was at the end of the evening's play on his farewell
visit while they sat drinking vodka, that Carol leaned
forward and said:

"I shall miss you—both of you. You must know that
I have been at home here—a word I have rarely been
able to use to describe my own dwelling places."

It was almost a formal expression of gratitude, yet
awkward because it was impelled by genuine feelings.

When both husband and wife murmured some plati-
tude in reply, Carol looked at Elenutza and continued
quietly:

"Tell me this: why is a prince cursed all the time with
flattery or insults?"

She gazed at him thoughtfully.

"Perhaps it is because your position inevitably causes
jealous hatred," she replied at length. "Whether you get
subservience or adulation, it is really the same thing. You
must know the Rumanian proverb—'He who flatters has
either just cheated you or is about to do so'."

Carol rose to go.

"At least in this house I have been safe from cheats," he
said.

At the door he shook hands with his brother officer and
then bent to kiss the hand of his hostess.

Her skin was soft and warm, and he felt her fingers
tremble against his. His lips lingered overlong before she
stiffened imperceptibly and he sensed the warning to desist.

He straightened himself and they smiled convention-
ally. But there was a hidden fire deep in the darkness of

their eyes. They were both conscious of a tingling excitement and magnetism passing between them.

Neither of them ever forgot that moment of deep and intimate understanding. Both knew that a message had flashed between them, and that they would always remember the sensation which had thrilled them both so that their hearts beat faster and their pulses throbbed whenever they thought of it.

Carol had fallen in love with a married woman. And she knew, with a woman's intuition, that her future, for good or ill, would be inextricably linked to his.

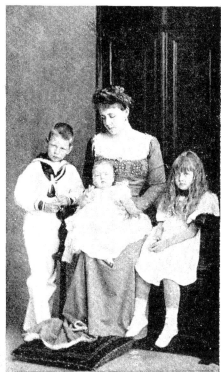

(Right) Carol at the age of seven with his mother and his two sisters, Elizabetta, aged six, and the baby Marie.

(Left) A woman whose romantic mind and tragic life deeply affected Carol as a child—his great-aunt, Queen Elizabeth, whose poems and essays (under the name of Carmen Sylva) were internationally known.

Photos: Popper-Handke Collection)

(*Left*) The man Carol "neither loved nor was loved by"—his father, King Ferdinand.

(*Below*) Carol's mother, Queen Marie, in her favourite "peasant dress".

(*Photo: Mansell Collection*)

5

1920

THE Crown Prince left on his world tour. It was launched with a very quiet send-off compared with the publicised junketings that followed once he was out of the country.

Before he left, Carol sent a piece of small but expensive jewellery to Elenutza, together with a note that left no doubt as to his feelings for her.

Elenutza kept the letter to herself, but as she loved jewellery and had little of any value, she could not resist wearing the brooch. Her husband, of course, noticed it and when he asked where she had got it from, she made no pretence about the identity of the donor.

With a lively knowledge of his royal friend's romantic proclivities, Captain Tempeanu was a little worried. But not unduly so.

Moral standards in post-war Rumanian society were lax, and strangely enough the licence did not apply only to the menfolk. Whatever jealousy might be aroused in a husband's breast by his wife's infidelities, he would get only smiling sympathy from friends and acquaintances. The erring wife ran virtually no risk of social ostracism provided her choice of lover was not someone too uncouth or poor.

The Rumanian temperament was a mixture of East and West. On the one hand was an Oriental fatality with regard to human emotions and the inadvisable actions they bred. On the other a fervid anxiety to be Western and 'modern' precluded any retrograde attitude towards the freedom of women, whether married or single. The general view was that a cuckolded husband should balance matters by finding someone else's wife for his own emotional comfort.

Consequently, although the Captain was convinced that his wife's appeal to Carol would, when opportunity arose, develop through flirtation into an 'affaire', he did not know what to do about it.

In any event, Carol was his superior officer and his future king. As a professional soldier, even the mildest of protests or the least gesture towards defending his honour might bring disaster. Captain Tempeanu tried to believe Elenutza's assurances that nothing amatory had so far occurred. He comforted himself with the knowledge that Carol was to be out of the country for almost a year. He knew his Royal friend well enough to believe that there was no question of Carol remaining faithful to a memory.

He kept the information about the gift of jewellery to himself. If he had thought that this ensured secrecy he was strangely unaware of the efficient espionage services of both the Court and the Army. Although Carol had personally bought the brooch in a small shop in Bucharest, although the gift had been despatched in the care of a messenger he regarded as absolutely loyal, the news of the gift and the name of the person to whom it had been given were on King Ferdinand's desk within a few hours.

The name Elenutza Tempeanu meant to the police a many-paged dossier, although most of it was motiveless information. In extremely secret papers filed among the personal documents of the King the name also existed, and the details were voluminous, although no additions had been made for some years.

The army's security services were ordered to investigate the life of the Tempeanus. The Royal cipher on the memorandum stirred the agents to activity. But the material on file on Captain Tempeanu was routine and not of any particular interest. Anxious to please, officers were posted to Bistrita and began enquiries about Elenutza.

By the time Carol had arrived at Bombay and was basking in an ostentatious official welcome by the British authorities and enjoying the private delights available with the guidance of a few Rajahs and minor Indian princes, the dossier was ready.

It reported that Captain Tempeanu had been a personal friend of the Crown Prince for five years and that since his marriage, Madame Tempeanu had been favoured with a share of this friendship. It gave details of the parties at the Tempeanu house over the previous six months, listing the guests whether Carol was among them or not. It described in detail the brooch which Elenutza was now wearing.

Normally the material would merely have been filed away with other dossiers on the women who had, for an hour, a night, or a week, enjoyed princely favour. It might have been closed with no more details than those obtained on Zizi Lambrino. But long before Elenutza joined the short and notorious roster of Royal mistresses who have changed the course of history, long before any real intimacy developed between her and Carol, the King had ordered a special watch to be kept on her every activity. This meant an examination of every letter in or out of the Tempeanu household, and the placing of an agent as a servant in her home.

The reason was a bizarre one, known only to a select handful of officials whose loyalty to the throne exceeded beyond question their devotion to the State.

The official files on Elenutza Tempeanu's life and background went back for nearly a hundred years. They described her grandfather as a Jew named Wolff, a member of the strictly orthodox Jewish community which had taken refuge from the Russian pogroms in Poland by settling in Jassy. There a son was born, who worked for an apothecary and in due course opened a shop of his own.

Shortly after he was twenty-one he went to Vienna for

business reasons. There he met a Viennese girl and, despite the fact that she was a Catholic, married her.

The young man had possibly painted to his bride a glowing picture of his prosperous apothecary shop in Jassy. It was, in fact, a poverty-stricken business in a desperately poor section of the Ghetto. Marriage did not make life any easier for him.

The bride was a deeply religious woman, despite her almost unforgivable sin in marrying out of her faith, and even out of the Christian religion. Her husband had committed business suicide in bringing a Gentile into his house. The trickle of customers almost dried up, and Wolff was compelled to make an abrupt change.

Although he never denied his religion he took the surname of Lupescu. It was one which was popular among his race when it was necessary to identify themselves with the people of the country in which they had taken refuge. Ostracised by both Gentile and Jew for the heinous offence of their marriage, the young couple started a new business outside the Ghetto and managed to scrape a living.

Somehow—and the ordinary police dossier offered no solution on the point—Lupescu was able to ignore the vicious anti-Semitic laws of the latter half of the nineteenth century which prohibited Jews from owning or working in Rumanian apothecary shops.

His shop was permitted to survive, although there was no evidence that he had bribed the town's officials to get a permit nor had he taken out Rumanian naturalisation papers. The official concerned could have made the normal issue of a permit possible simply by ignoring the details of the applicant's religion. He was either extraordinarily lucky in evading the repercussions of universal loathing of his marriage or he had powerful allies far above the petty autocrats of Jassy.

Soon after the new premises were opened, the first and only child of the union was born—Elenutza. The year

· was 1897, when war broke out between Turkey and Greece. Through his fear of hostilities spreading into the Balkans, or possibly for the more direct motive of starting life once again in more amenable surroundings, Lupescu moved to Sulina.

It was a dreary little port on the marshy coastline where the Danube meandered across the plains and emptied itself into the Black Sea. It could provide, if necessary, an easy escape to Russia where Lupescu had relatives; and this, it was thought by the Rumanian official Intelligence, was really the reason for his abrupt and difficult move from Jassy.

There all information about Madame Lupescu ended. Whether she died, returned to her own family, or was sent to her husband's relatives, was a mystery. She apparently remained under her husband's roof long enough to care for Elenutza through infancy and see her enter a Convent school.

That the child should have been brought up in the Catholic faith was to be expected. But the ability of this impecunious apothecary to arrange his child's admission to one of the finest Convents in Bucharest or indeed, the whole of the Balkans was inexplicable.

Nevertheless, as the documents of the Bucharest police showed with ample proof, Elenutza Lupescu had been approved as a scholar of this distinguished academy. It meant that her religious background was regarded as without blemish, for the convent was run on the strictest Catholic regimen. It insinuated that socially she was comparable to the children of the oldest and most aristocratic families in Rumania.

This was judged by standards set down by the German-born staff of the place and not on the easier and more broad-minded conception of ancestry prevalent among the politically powerful Rumanian families.

King Carol I, fervently anxious to create an aura of distinction around the throne, had personally watched over the progress of the school. He believed that by the time Ferdinand came to the throne he would, with the convent's help, have created a matriarchy for Rumanian society. It was to be Prussian-like in its unbending regard for convention, virtuous through the accent on Catholicism, exclusive because only birth and breeding would count.

The happy-go-lucky temperament of the Rumanians, encouraged by the corruptive influence of the Bratianu oligarchy, had minimised the effect of this scheme. But it had undoubtedly, in a single generation, created a focal point of envy for the rich and the powerful. In fact, it was the one and only background for an aristocratic Rumanian which could not be bought by money or influence. There was therefore no reason to suppose that the red-haired Elenutza Lupescu was not entirely acceptable to the convent.

So ended the inscribed facts about the child and her parentage. From the day Elenutza entered the Convent until she emerged a lovely and intelligent girl of eighteen she did nothing which merited any addition to the dossier. In the upheaval of war her marriage to a lieutenant of the Chasseur Regiment in 1915, when she was twenty-two, had been added only as a hastily scrawled footnote.

Where the facts ended there began a tornado of whispered rumours to explain the anomalies and para-doxes of this remarkable tale. There was not a policeman in Rumania who would not instantly have recognised the need for a dossier on this wife of an obscure army captain in a distant garrison town.

Her Jewish father had married a Catholic wife, despite laws and customs which made such a union impossible in theory and improbable in practice. Her mother's anonymity and subsequent disappearance from the narrative aroused the most piquant rumination. The unsuccessful apothecary's ability to move his business from one town to another suggested connivance by the authorities, while the major mystery of all was the girl's admission to a school which demanded money, nobility, an impeccable background, and Royal approval.

Secret as the dossiers on Elenutza ostensibly were, a thousand prying eyes in government departments, police bureaux and army headquarters had over the years read through them.

Wisely these minions of law and order ensured that their superiors knew nothing of their prying. According to the type of their personal phobias one name after another came up for whispered discussion, for sniggering innuendo and bawdy jokes.

Now with their wives, their drinking cronies and their colleagues, they discussed the entrancing possibilities that lay behind the queer history of the Jewish apothecary and his daughter. It was not strange that the spicy theories discussed and accepted eddied out from Bucharest and Jassy as a scandalous rumour which dripped its insidious way into a myriad of memories.

The first and most universal suggestion was that Madame Lupescu had been the daughter of an important branch of the Rumanian nobility. She had fallen in love with Wolff Lupescu and, when family castigation failed to make her change her mind, a marriage had been arranged. The fortunate bridegroom had been given financial assistance and facilities to obtain Rumanian citizenship so long as he kept his mouth shut.

The eagerness of the bride's family to show such consideration could have been due solely to the fact that the girl was already pregnant. A principal clause in the contract ensured that the Jewish father should not stand in the way of his child's education which should be decided entirely by his parents-in-law.

It was a feasible story in some ways. Among the bourgeoisie of Rumania, similar examples could be found in hundreds of families. Scores of men and women accused of Jewish origin had escaped the vile persecutions which besmirched the country's history because they could prove similar connections with pure Rumanian blood.

But there were also insurmountable snags to the tale. A family of real nobility or of political power commensurate with that of even a minor branch of the Bratianu dynasty would easily have found a more acceptable husband for a pregnant daughter than an obscure Jew. And if the girl had been so unwise as to refuse a selected bridegroom and to insist on public recognition of her seducer, the Jew would have been forced to emigrate. Or it was even more likely he would have simply disappeared and the local police would have been advised not to investigate his absence too closely.

Even if all these expected solutions of an amatory problem were jettisoned there still remained the unbending and inflexible Carol I and Ferdinand. The former would have never authorised the child's admittance to the Convent, or the latter, when he came to the throne, would have had her thrown out.

The Mother Superior of the Convent, the consulting priests, and the sisters who taught the girls, were ostensibly answerable to God alone. But their Prussian background told them that their mission was to serve their Deity as disciplinarians of girls whose background, environment and character were without social blemish in the eyes of their secular adviser—the ordained monarch of the land in which they worked.

Among thinking people, therefore, the Bratianu maternal theory was dismissed, and along with it went a more romantic one of a Bratianu with a conscience who had moved heaven and earth to provide for his love child. This idea was only put forward as a joke. The bastards of the aristocracy were legion, and no one could really believe that any one of them would get singled out for such unique treatment.

The rumour that Elenutza had Royal blood in her veins was akin to dynamite. The mere repetition of such a slanderous story would have been regarded as treason against the Rumanian throne and State. Probing further behind the bizarre details might bring sudden and terrible vengeance.

Nevertheless, its very salacity and intriguing possibilities exerted a mesmeric influence on the romantic Rumanian mind so that many contributed their own findings to the pool of evidence.

First and foremost, the theory of Royal paternity for the girl immediately answered the query as to why a more or less meaningless dossier had been meticulously compiled during the offices of a succession of Governments. This was really the major mystery of the whole business. Why else should the life story of a young girl occupy the files devoted to soldiers, politicians, foreign agents, and diplomats who had all spent a lifetime in political intrigue of varying degrees of patriotism or treachery ?

There was a story which, for years before Carol began to be interested in Elenutza had been whispered around the drawing-rooms, Government offices and cafés of Bucharest.

It began in the last decade of the nineteenth century when Carol I was already past middle age. This austere and unhappy man had only one real passion in life: a love of trees. When talking of arboriculture he became animated and human. Only a few people knew of him like this, but among them were the peasant farmers and labourers in the district of Scroviste Peris, where he had a private farm and estate.

Carol I spent as much time as he could there, supervising his plantations and very often himself digging and hewing. In all Rumania perhaps only the easy-going and friendly people on his estate and among the neighbouring farms saw the man rather than the monarch.

There was deep sympathy among them for his personal sorrows as well as a recognition of his knowledge as a

specialised farmer. Carol I was not living with his wife, the
Queen Elizabeth who preferred to be known to the world
as Carmen Sylva—a preference which in itself damned
her in the eyes of a man who regarded the monarchy as
divine.

The hostility that had come between them was of
tragic origin. Their only child had died at the age of three
after a birth which chronically injured the mother. Doctors
stated that any further children were improbable while
the unlikely conception would bring about a most
dangerous situation.

The Royal couple had perforce ceased to live as man
and wife. Incompatibility became complete when the
neurotic and frustrated Queen found solace in the company of a Bucharest writer and artist, Helen Vacarescu.
The King, disgusted by his wife's devotion and unques-
tioning adulation of this woman, banished for a time
both women from Rumania.

Queen and artist went to live in Venice where their
intimacy was better understood for what it was than by
the King. The latter's chief complaint against his wife had
been about her lowering of the Royal standards by her
friendship with a woman who was a commoner.

For Carol I this meant a life of terrible loneliness.
His Ministers neither wished nor dared to be friendly with
him. And his code of behaviour was so strict that a mistress in the palace was out of the question.

But, in those dangerous years for a man, the early
fifties, he fell deeply in love. The object of his affections
was the school teacher in the village near his estate. In
her late twenties, she came from a local family whose
ancestors had been Boyars and she had attained her quite
considerable intellectual standard by sheer hard work.

The King got into the habit of stopping and talking to
her on his morning stroll down the village street. He
asked about the conduct and attainments of her pupils,
whose parents were, of course, well known to him.

He found pleasure in the gentle conversation of this educated woman. Then sometimes, as he walked on a summer's evening around his tree seedlings, he would meet her with her lover. The man was an assistant to the village apothecary who, it was said, had gone bankrupt after trying to run his own business in Jassy.

King Carol would greet them in friendly fashion, talk for a little while, then pass on.

There came the evening when the King took his accustomed walk, half hoping for the bitter sweet joy of seeing the woman he loved with the man to whom she was betrothed. To his surprise she approached in the gathering twilight—alone.

It was the autumn of 1896. The darkness was falling earlier every evening. Soon there would be no more tree planting in the frost-hardened ground. But before Carol I left to resume the cares of kingship he knew that the little school teacher of Scroviste Peris was expecting his child.

A German-born A.D.C., whose loyalty and discretion to the King's person was above reproach, arranged everything. The apothecary's assistant was invited to earn unique privileges for a Jew. There would be Rumanian citizenship, money to re-open his business in Jassy, Royal protection for his family and himself for life. With loyal co-operation existence could become easy for him, but the slightest divergence from discretion would bring down on his head terrible and fatal consequences.

The marriage took place in the local church. From the Patriarch, a personal friend of the King as well as official adviser and helpmeet, came an order to the local priest on threat of excommunication to omit from his records all details of the ceremony. The bridal pair set off for Jassy within twenty-four hours of their wedding, and no one in Scroviste Peris gave them another thought after a month or so had passed. Certainly they never learned of the birth of a daughter seven months later.

In Jassy the disloyalty of Wolff to his race and religion in changing his name to Lupescu and marrying a Gentile meant he was ostracised by his Jewish friends. For the same reason the Rumanians who were his neighbouring shopkeepers never became friendly enough to probe into the couple's private background. To make doubly sure of secrecy, there soon came another generous gift of money, and the Lupescus with their baby disappeared Eastwards.

The story, facile and credible as it might be, could not by its very nature be backed up with a tittle of tangible evidence. The school teacher seemed to have vanished. Her husband was very much alive, but resisted all attempts to make him talk.

He merely confirmed what everyone knew—that his daughter had lived nearly all her life at the Convent. When anyone was rude enough to suggest that his ancestry did not warrant such an honour, he would grin slyly, and say: "It's simply disgraceful what money can do nowadays."

There was no record of a marriage in the Scroviste Peris church ledger, no record either there or in Jassy of the naturalisation of a Jew called Lupescu. The very nothingness of official and public data on the lives of the apothecary's assistant and the school teacher was in itself positive evidence in the opinion of many people.

There remained one telling item to support the theory of these rumour-mongers. Those who had seen Elenutza Lupescu after she left the convent or when she became a war-time bride of Lieutenant Tempeanu could give a verbal portrait of her lovely face, her proud carriage, and her charming mannerisms.

Their listeners may not have ever seen the girl, but many had seen a contemporary to whom almost exactly the same description could have been applied.

Elenutza Lupescu might have been the twin sister of Princess Elizabetta, sister of Crown Prince Carol, and grand-niece of the late Carol I.

6

1920 – 1921

WHILE the Rumanian Court worried itself about the potential danger of Elenutza Lupescu, the Crown Prince was causing fresh trouble by his antics abroad.

After the first of his official engagements in India, he disappeared for some weeks into the independent states of the Maharajas and Rajas, where he spent a pleasant time hunting tiger. There were banquets in the evenings at which Carol introduced his hosts to the delights of Russian champagne. Large supplies of this wine had been sent by his special order in a sequence of ships after he himself arrived in India.

Alarming reports were received by the Rumanian Court of the Crown Prince's behaviour in the less desirable night haunts of the larger cities of India and of the wild parties which were arranged at his request by his Indian hosts.

These reports came from Rumanian diplomatic sources in India and also from the British authorities who let it be known that Carol's behaviour was causing them some embarrassment. It was obvious that the tour, designed to broaden the Prince's outlook and give him a sense of responsibility, had, in fact, merely increased his independence and brought out still further the unpleasant traits of self-indulgence in his character.

An order was cabled from Bucharest insisting that Carol should continue his world tour. Unwillingly he embarked at Calcutta for Japan. But *en route* he visited Singapore and once again there were accounts of his nocturnal activities on pleasure bent.

Eventually he reached his destination where he had a definite diplomatic duty to carry out on behalf of his father. This was to convey a message of good wishes to the Nipponese Son of Heaven.

Carol was always impressed by spectacle so long as he himself was the focal point of it, and for a time in Tokio, where he was treated with the full majesty due to his birth and rank, he behaved with some decorum.

The visit to Japan was in fact both diplomatically and commercially successful, and resulted in considerable benefit to both countries in the promotion of trade. This was, however, of little interest to the world's press which was almost entirely preoccupied with the more private antics of Carol during his absence from home.

With growing alarm the Rumanian Government and his parents realised that from a personal point of view, the tour had been a dismal failure. Carol was ordered to return by the most direct route possible, and accommodation was provided for him on a ship which stopped at Eastern ports for only the briefest periods.

Queen Marie was a resourceful woman, and even though she spent many sleepless nights worrying over her son, she would not admit defeat. She knew instinctively that the real danger to her son's stability lay in Rumania itself, and the most likely source of danger was in the little home at Jassy where Madame Tempeanu lived.

The Queen had many discreet conversations with Ministers on whom she believed she could rely. One of them in discussing the reaction of the Rumanian people to any rumoured romantic liaison between the Crown Prince and the officer's wife remarked: "If this woman, Elenutza, had been the illegitimate child of a Bucharest prostitute, they would not have minded at all. It would have appealed greatly to their sense of romance. If, however, as report seems to have it, she is of Jewish blood, they will loathe her."

After the audience had ended, Queen Marie pondered

on this point for a long time. She saw in it a possible means of stopping any chance of the people rallying to Carol's side should the worst occur and the liaison become open knowledge among the ordinary citizens of town and country.

It was from this moment that the story got abroad that Elenutza was definitely of Jewish origin.

Queen Marie, with little faith in the ability of the Government to do much about her son's welfare, saw in a twist of fate a remarkable opportunity to remedy matters once and for all.

For some years there had been a genuine romantic interest between Carol's eldest sister, Elizabetta, and the Crown Prince of Greece. During the war there had been many reasons why no marriage could be arranged, but as soon as Queen Marie recognised the possibilities, through this marriage, of bringing about a union of her own Royal House and that of Greece, she eagerly pushed the arrangements forward.

While the ship bringing Carol home was still at sea, he received a cable from his mother asking him to go to Switzerland and from there to accompany Prince George of Greece to Rumania, in order that the formal engagement could be celebrated. Carol, of course, could see no ulterior motive in this and sent back the reply that he was agreeable to do what was asked. After the ship docked at Marseilles, he made his way direct to Lucerne, where Prince George was awaiting him.

The Greek royal family was at the time in exile, and as well as his son, Prince George, King Constantine also had his daughters Helen and Irene living with him in the town beside the lake. As soon as Queen Marie learned that Carol had arrived, she sent a telegram inviting the two girls to accompany their brother to Bucharest in order to take part in the celebrations.

Helen had no desire to accept the invitation. She was an extremely reserved girl more interested in games and physical fitness than in any of the usual activities of a Royal Princess.

She was, indeed, heartily sick of everything connected with the throne, because she had seen only too clearly the misery which occurred when a king sat insecurely on it. Her father, however, was extremely pleased at the invitation from the Queen of Rumania because, as he said, "It will show the world that even though I am treated as a pariah, my children are not."

A special train with coaches decorated with the Royal Insignia of Rumania was sent to Lucerne, and after a few days during which Carol was merely taciturn when in the presence of his guests, the party set off for Bucharest.

During the journey the Greek royal family saw nothing whatever of the Crown Prince, who kept to his own private coach. At the last moment the train was redirected from the capital of Rumania to Sinaia, in the North, as the royal family were at the Pelishor. It was late October and the autumn was unusually fine.

Princess Helen was extremely happy in the beautiful estates which surrounded both the Pelishor and the larger Pelesh Castle which lay a mile or two beyond it. Occasionally, when she was walking or riding through the forests, she would see Carol with an adjutant in the distance, but always the Prince, riding off at a gallop, deliberately avoided her.

His behaviour was almost insulting. Queen Marie's elaborate plans seemed doomed to failure.

News came that Helen's brother, Alexander, had died in Athens and shortly after that, that Queen Marie's mother, the Duchess of Edinburgh, had also died suddenly. There was a railway strike in Rumania, and for a time it was impossible to make any arrangements to leave for the funeral.

However, when Queen Marie set out for Coburg where her mother's body lay in state, she insisted on taking Prince George, his fiancée and Helen with her. She was so disheartened at the sullen behaviour of Carol that, for once, she did not even suggest that he should come. Typical of his quixotic character, he demanded at the last moment that he should join the party.

The route of the Royal train was once again via Switzerland, and this time Carol's attitude to the Greek princess was diametrically opposite to that of the journey to Rumania. He paid gallant attentions to her, showed her how able he was as a conversationalist and how charming a companion he could be.

The fact was that although this love-hungry young man realised what were his mother's plans, he was deliberately trying to fall in love with Helen. What was more, he succeeded in doing so. Gone were Carol's intentions of escorting Queen Marie to Coburg for the funeral. He remained in Lucerne, re-joining the exiled Greek family there.

After a few days he suggested to Helen that they should make a brief tour of the scenic beauties of Northern Switzerland. There they spent long hours together, with Carol at the wheel of a hired car driving at break-neck speed along the mountain roads.

On the day that his mother was due to return, and they were all to take the train to Rumania, Carol went to see ex-King Constantine and formally asked for his daughter's hand in marriage. Constantine replied that he would prefer to know Helen's feelings before he gave a direct answer.

It was probably true that Helen was more in love with love than with Carol. This had been the first time in her life that she had enjoyed any sort of freedom with a person of the other sex and of her own age. For her the few hours sitting beside Carol in that car, enjoying a drink in a tiny café and climbing the easier slopes of the mountains, had been of unbelievable charm.

Helen told her father that she felt deeply happy that Carol wanted to marry her. The ex-King answered that the decision was entirely hers. By his lack of enthusiasm, his daughter, had she been more sophisticated, might have known that he was worried about the engagement.

On the other hand, her mother's feelings were expressed freely. The ex-Queen wept openly when she heard the news, and on the evening after Carol had seen Constantine, she pleaded with Helen for an hour, using every argument and blandishment to make her think again. She even warned her that Carol's reputation precluded any real chance of happiness for them both.

When Queen Marie returned from Coburg she was naturally overjoyed to hear what had happened, and in her usual domineering way she easily overruled any doubts that Helen's mother had aroused. It was as if there were happy auguries all around.

While Helen and Carol continued their holiday together in Switzerland, the news came that by an overwhelming majority the Greek people had voted for the restoration of the monarchy. By late November the Greek royal family were on the way to Venice where a Greek cruiser was to take them back to their country in triumph.

Carol's parting with Helen was an affectionate one. At Lucerne station he kissed her openly, holding her hand as she stood at the carriage door, and begging her not to leave it too long before she came to see him in Rumania. Queen Marie watched them, her face alight with happiness for the first time for many years.

One of the first announcements made by the King of Greece when he returned to the throne, was that of the engagement of his daughter to the Crown Prince of Rumania. It was agreed that the marriage should take place in March.

Helen did not accompany her brother George when he was married to Elizabetta in Bucharest at the beginning of the month, but a day or two after the ceremony Carol arrived in Athens and once again there was an idyllic period when she showed him the chief sights of the city and the neighbourhood.

Just as the autumn in Switzerland had been unusually fine, so the spring in Greece was remarkably early. It was as if even the weather prophesied their future happiness.

As the day of the wedding drew near, however, Helen began to have second thoughts. There were awkward hours when she felt that Carol was a complete stranger and there were certainly moments when the intensity of his love-making frankly terrified her. She began to be unsure of herself and of her love. This was partly because she was now back in her own country, and the sense of loneliness that had been so acute in Switzerland had naturally disappeared. However, the day of the wedding was now very near, and it was clearly impossible for her to go back on her word.

On 10th March, 1921, Carol of Rumania and Helen of Greece were married in the Metropolitan Cathedral of Athens. The wedding ceremony of the Greek Orthodox Church was long and elaborate. It was noted by the congregation that the bridegroom became frankly bored with the involved ritual, while in contrast the bride seemed to gain great strength from the solemn religious blessings on the union. When Helen left the Cathedral on her husband's arm and entered the golden coach which headed the procession, she looked radiant with an almost spiritual loveliness.

The Athenians lining the streets were wildly excited about the marriage. It was the first wedding of a Princess of Greece ever to have taken place in the city. They noted, however, in surprise that the bridegroom was morose and looked straight ahead of him.

After the wedding breakfast and State reception at the Royal Palace, Carol drove his bride away to Tatoi, the beautiful mountain residence which the King of Greece normally used during the summer.

The honeymoon lasted only a week, and the bridal

pair returned to Athens where Carol more and more
frequently went off on his own. His excuse was that he
wished, while he had the opportunity, to see the archaeo-
logical remains of the country, and also to gather spring
flowers for his collection. It was perfectly true that he had
a genuine interest in botany and a considerable knowledge
of it, but this sudden enthusiasm for his hobby a week or
ten days after his wedding, hardly seemed to be in
character.

It was at this time that he made a curious remark to a
member of his personal staff when they were inspecting
the ruins around the Parthenon.

"You know," he said, "my bride has considerable
understanding for my battered heart and shares completely my views on life."

If Carol really meant this, he was sadly wrong about
Helen. The whole difficulty was that even if she had some
identity of interests with him, she certainly did not understand his heart. A timid, unemotional girl, Carol's fiery
love-making failed to awaken any answering passion in
her.

The honeymoon was—and they both knew it—a
terrible disillusionment. Carol suggested that it was high
time that they returned to Rumania, although up to then
it had been agreed by the Royal parents on both sides
that the honeymoon should continue throughout the
summer, with possibly at the end an intimate cruise
through the Aegean.

Helen did not wish to leave her homeland, but when
Carol dropped very strong hints that he intended to go to
Bucharest whether she came or not, she had to give way.

At the beginning of May a ship of the Rumanian State
Lines arrived to transport them. It passed by the islands
of the Aegean—which it had been thought would be the
scene of many happy hours for the honeymoon couple—
through the Dardanelles and across the Sea of Marmora
towards Constantinople. After a short stay in the ancient

city, the ship journeyed through the Bosphorus, and across the Black Sea to Constanta.

Carol was unusually quiet as they sat on deck acknowledging the cheers of the crowd on the quayside of the Rumanian port. He was back at the scene of another projected royal romance in his life, that of his meeting with the Tsar and his family in 1916. Then also he had been ready to comply with his Royal duties, and had been hopeful that he could find genuine love to make it easier to carry them out.

Now he had returned to the little town married to a woman who was acceptable to his people, his government, and his family. He smiled to himself a little when he thought how well he had carried out the duties of a Prince—better even than the mob on the quay realised.

Although they had been married less than two months, Helen already knew that she would bear a child.

The journey in the royal train from Constanta to Bucharest was the beginning of a great ordeal for the new Crown Princess. As she looked out of the window she saw groups of peasants standing near the line, most of them in their National costume and waving excitedly as the train passed. Carol's marriage had caused spontaneous excitement among the romantic Rumanian people, quite apart from the careful efforts of Queen Marie to make it a popular occasion.

Helen was unaccustomed to such scenes of adulation, and as the train neared Bucharest, she became more and more nervous.

There the full ceremony began. On the platform, King Ferdinand and Queen Marie, as well as other members of the royal family, stood waiting. Nearby were the chief ministers of state, dignitaries of the church, and large numbers of troops. Carol escorted his bride to an open carriage, and the procession through the streets of Bucharest to the Cotroceni Palace began.

The loud cheers of the huge crowds which lined the

streets changed to murmurs as they noticed how wooden-faced Helen sat in the carriage. At times Carol leant towards her and whispered, evidently trying to tell her at least to smile and acknowledge the people.

It was no fault of Helen's that she was quite unable to give any impression of happiness. Never in her life had she been a centre of interest in this way and she was frankly frightened by the noise and the prominence in which she found herself.

Before the state luncheon, Queen Marie, who under-stood the reasons for her new daughter-in-law's strange behaviour, begged her to try to overcome her shyness and make herself more pleasant. Try as she would the girl could not do so. The speeches were in Rumanian—not a word of which she understood—and as the various people ranging from the chief ministers of state to peasants representing small communities in different parts of the country came forward and presented her with addresses of welcome and gifts, she became more and more uneasy.

Shyness is one thing which no Rumanian really under-stands. He is a friendly, exuberant person and expects everybody to be the same. As a result, the Princess's reserved behaviour was regarded as an indication that she was unhappy. The belief that this was really a true romance disappeared almost over-night, and the whis-perings began that an arranged marriage would certainly not cure the Crown Prince of his romantic interests elsewhere.

For a fortnight, Helen had to endure a life in which she was hardly ever absent from official functions. Queen Marie had provided a suite of apartments in the Cotroceni Palace, and at every meal, except breakfast, there were various people for her to meet.

Realising that a crisis was already approaching, Queen Marie suggested that perhaps the bridal couple would like to resume the privacy of a honeymoon and move to the small chalet in the grounds of Pelesh Castle known as the Foishor.

The building itself was pretty, but the interior was enough to intimidate any young girl. It had been built for King Carol I as a sort of summer-house to which he could retire during his happier days with his Queen. Eccentric Carmen Sylva had furnished it in her own peculiar taste. The decorations were frankly appalling, and as the place had not been used in any way for at least five years, it was also in very bad condition.

Helen asked Carol if arrangements could be made to clean the whole place out and refurnish it with more modern furniture.

Strangely enough, he became furiously angry about this, the reason possibly being that he had been very fond of his half-mad great aunt. In his refusal to change anything, he was backed up by the King and Queen, who also wished that the place should be kept much as it had always been. Helen resigned herself to living in an atmosphere that she loathed.

Her daily existence almost immediately became deeply unhappy. She was quite unsuited emotionally to her marriage, and her amorous and highly sexed husband soon became more and more impatient with her. Also on the orders of the King even the most intimate meal at the Foishor had to be organised like a State banquet.

The royal couple sat at either end of an immense table and studied menus on which the items of food were printed in gold. The meals lasted interminably.

Helen could not have guessed that Carol's tastes were really remarkably simple. He did, in fact, prefer the ordinary little meals which had been prepared by Zizi or even the more intricate menus which he had been offered at the home of the Tempeanus. But at the Foishor, he neither had the intimacy of an understanding woman nor the comforts of a smoothly run royal household to which he had been accustomed when his mother was in charge. He began to make frequent excuses that it was necessary for him to go and see his Regiment at Sinaia.

In the middle of the summer, King Ferdinand and Queen Marie left for a foreign tour and Helen was for many hours, and later for days on end, left entirely alone. All she could do was to roam about the estate and explore the empty Pelesh Castle.

This was an immense and rambling building containing more than 150 rooms, most of which had been left exactly as they were when King Carol I died. The skeleton staff of servants in the castle began to chatter about the pathetic Princess who had no one with whom she could talk and was obviously extremely unhappy.

It was perhaps fortunate that Helen could not understand Rumanian, and was therefore safe from the busybodies who might have told her the truth about her husband. Quite a number of people knew that Carol had driven over the Transylvanian Mountains on the 160 miles of roads to Jassy, where once again he was seeing Elenutza Tempeanu.

He was not even in the house when on October 25th, 1921, Helen gave birth prematurely to a son.

The birth of the child, who was to be christened Michael, was, his mother thought, fraught with the signs of doom. He was born on the anniversary of the death of her brother the year before. It was all in a pattern with the unhappiness and tragedy which seemed to surround her life.

Helen was the grand-daughter of George I of Greece, who was murdered. She was the niece of the Kaiser, now a figure of contempt and pathos in exile in Holland. She was the cousin of the murdered Tsar of Russia.

Carol was in Jassy when he heard of the birth of his son. On the way back, while he rested during a minor repair to his car, a gypsy approached him. Like most Rumanians, he was intensely superstitious and had an implicit belief in the clairvoyant powers of the half-million Romany people who had for centuries inhabited the kingdom.

The old crone, who doubtless recognised the Prince, begged that her palm should be crossed with gold so that she could tell his fortune. He told her smilingly that that very morning he had become a father.

"Tell me," he said, "what fortune lies ahead for my son?"

The woman refused to answer the question, but looking at Carol straight in the face, muttered with an intensity that almost frightened him: "Without the woman you love you will die."

Carol gave her some money, got back in the car and drove on to the Foishor. He could not get the words of the gypsy woman out of his head. As he thought of them he faced the truth that the woman he loved was named Elenutza.

7

1921—1926

THE royal marriage, less than a year old, was by the early winter strained to breaking point. Queen Marie, thinking resignedly along the lines of "the young people might work things out successfully if they were left to themselves" tumbled on a solution. She suggested that they should have a private home of their own, away from the strict conventions of Court routine and free from innumerable prying eyes of courtiers and State servants.

Helen was delighted, Carol non-committal. Without being given any choice in the matter, the newly-weds were told that a small house in the fashionable Chaussée Kyself was available for them. The place, incidentally, had been approved by the Government because from the neighbouring residences a watch could be undertaken over Carol's comings and goings.

The place had a charming exterior. But inside conditions were hardly favourable for mending marital damage. Bits and pieces from various palaces had been sent by the Royal Comptroller without any regard for taste or comfort. Carol took one look inside and said that he would regard the house as merely an occasional lodging place until some better furnishings could be ordered from London.

Helen, who moved in with her son and the nurses from the now bitterly cold Foishor, did her best to create some homeliness out of the garish, old-fashioned and shabby Rumanian traditional furniture and the pretty but uncomfortable pieces bought forty years earlier in Paris and Vienna for royal reception rooms.

However, she soon gave up trying to make a home for a husband who rarely appeared. Shortly before Christmas in a desolation of lonely misery she requested permission to go to Athens to see her parents.

As the Crown Princess, she had to obtain formal permission from both the King and the Government to move anywhere. The fact that she wanted to take her son Michael with her aggravated the official objections to her plan.

But Queen Marie hoped that the virtually complete schism that now existed between her son and daughter-in-law might be disguised for a little longer if Helen were to go away on a holiday. She persuaded the King to authorise the trip as soon as Michael had been christened, at the same time making arrangements for a series of official duties for Carol to give the impression that he could not be spared.

Helen remained in Greece for four months. When the requests from Bucharest became more and more insistent that she should return she was also given the first inkling of the developments which had, during her absence, turned suspicion of Carol's infidelity into stark fact.

Carol had resumed his liaison with Elenutza openly. He had abandoned whatever discretion he had ever shown, and was now an embittered, vengeful man. Ignoring his own disgraceful behaviour to his bride, he told his friends that Helen had deliberately gone off to Greece in order to wean Michael from his affections.

Carol was as devoted to his baby as he was inconsiderate to his wife. It was useless for anyone to tell him that a baby less than six months old would be quite unaffected by not seeing his father for a few weeks. He mournfully insisted that Michael and he would henceforth be strangers.

Perhaps his cruellest gesture was to start calling his mistress by the Anglicised name of Helena. Friends and acquaintances were embarrassed when he would quote some words from "Helena's letter received this morning" or remark on some mannerism of "my Helena", his audience being quite unable at first to appreciate whether he was talking about his wife or his mistress.

The whole country rocked with spicy rumour of the new and blatant liaison. There were plenty of know-alls, of course, who hit the target of truth without being aware of it when they said that they had known of the friendship for more than a year or so. The scandal became a political weapon and Carol was once again a personality in the arena where the parties fought for future supremacy.

The paradoxical situation arose in which the Bratianu faction who were the kingmakers and most powerful cordon round the throne, and also the morally lax and ruthlessly corrupt section of Rumanian society, climbed on a pedestal and decried Carol as a future king.

They had recognised with alarm and despondency that the Crown Prince was of a resolute character, and that there was every likelihood that he would resist direction as a king with all the obstinacy that he now showed when told to observe the emotional conventions.

On the other side, simply because anything the Bratianus called black must be white, was the National Peasant Party. This group was led by Juliu Maniu, a genuine democrat, and a loyal subject of the monarchy with an inborn belief in the divine right of kings. He was also blessed with a Puritanical streak which was constantly impelling him to tilt a lance at the immorality of Rumanian society. While Maniu prayed for Carol's virtue, he was prepared to dismiss the story of Helena Tempeanu as exaggerated, or at any rate as the ephemeral peccadillo of a young man.

These powerful forces clashed violently. One side strove to disgust the nation with stories of Carol's perfidy to his wife and little son while at the same time upholding the dignity of the dynasty. The other attempted to dismiss the whole business as unimportant and to laud the Crown Prince as an illustrious ornament of the monarchy.

Behind them the third mysterious force which had always watched over Helena's life played its effective role. While the political parties sent their agents swarming into Jassy to discover intimate details of Helena's life, both with and without Carol, ostensibly reliable and authentic details of her activities began to eddy through Bucharest and the army officers' messes indicating that as a woman and as a wife she was above reproach.

Nothing could be unearthed by the hostile factions to contradict these reports. Helena Tempeanu was conducting herself discreetly. She maintained that golden silence which was to be her most remarkable trait throughout her career. Neither the venal journalists of the Rumanian press, nor the independent American and British correspondents, who wanted nothing but the facts for a human love story, could get a word out of her, or—more important—a compromising word about her.

As discreetly and as efficiently as she had been admitted to the Convent school, permitted to marry an officer, left alone when Carol first showed an interest in her, her divorce was now put through.

Captain Tempeanu provided her with grounds to obtain her freedom. A divorce for an uninfluential Rumanian was in itself surprising; a divorce which did not immediately smash a junior officer's army career was a phenomenon.

But Captain Tempeanu seems to have found no difficulty in having his marital bonds legally untied without any prejudice to his career. Immediately afterwards he faded from the scene in a comfortable post for a senior army officer in the provinces.

Helena emerged from the divorce case with her virtue and reputation unscathed. She resumed her maiden name of Lupescu and was apparently well equipped financially for her new life—to an extent which, it was thought by those who knew Carol's income and expenditure to the nearest lei, excluded the possibility that he was supporting her.

While this pattern of the lives of Carol and Helena was being etched for the future, Princess Helen made her belated return to the villa on the Chaussée Kyselef. She brought her sister Irene with her, an understandable move to combat the loneliness she expected and dreaded, but not the wisest one if she had hoped against hope to heal the breach between Carol and herself.

The summer heat gave Carol the excuse to get away from the Bucharest villa. Helen, her baby, and her sister went to the Foishor again, where Carol appeared so occasionally that he was little more than a visitor. He also hurt his wife's pride by doing his utmost to arrange that he should not ride with her in the long delayed Coronation procession to celebrate the birth of Greater Rumania.

The growing sympathy of thousands of Rumanians for the Princess was greatly weakened by her cold and remote attitude during the Coronation festivities, so reminiscent of her behaviour when she arrived as a bride. She hardly managed to acknowledge the crowds, and during the service of dedication in the Cathedral of Alba Julia it was noticed that she was almost in tears.

The reason, if the Rumanian people could have forgotten their own festive happiness for a moment, would have been easy to discover. Helen's father had been forced once more to abdicate and was living in exile in Palermo.

Helen, trying to hold tenaciously to the only source of affection she had—her own family—had begged King Ferdinand that she should be permitted to go to her father. The King would not hear of it, insisting, as was perfectly reasonable, that she must attend the Coronation ceremonies first.

Later, the deeply worried Queen Marie did her best

to persuade Carol to go to Sicily with his wife, because she hoped against hope that it might weaken the Lupescu liaison. He was adamant in his refusal. He was equally insistent that this time Michael should be left behind.

Helen, perhaps foolishly, although she may have had a woman's instinctive knowledge that nothing remained of her marriage to save, still impatiently demanded permission to go without husband or son. Unwillingly it was granted.

The sorrow that had surrounded her since birth continued in its predestined pattern. She saw that her father was suffering more seriously than anyone else suspected. His gaunt and ageing body was not merely stricken by the disaster that had returned after so brief a respite, his physical health was also deteriorating rapidly. On January 11th, 1923, he dropped dead as he was dressing.

Helen stayed on at Palermo for a time, trying to accept the fact that the last haven of her life had gone. Resignedly she returned to Bucharest—and to the petty hell that Carol had created for her in their loveless home.

The embarrassment of their false lives, deeply felt by Helen but apparently of no consequence to Carol, was heightened because of the necessity of carrying out State functions. Sometimes they had to appear together, and then the obvious coldness of the Prince fanned the flames of rumour still brighter. If they appeared singly, the result was just the same.

"How long will it go on?" the Princess asked herself. "Surely it must end soon; this sort of thing cannot be tolerated for ever."

The end was nearer than she could have guessed. Suspicion of a foreigner, misunderstanding of her retiring personality, and the popularity of Carol with the masses resulted in the lonely young wife being treated with harshness.

Even Queen Marie chided her for failing to attract her son as a loving wife should be able to do. King

Ferdinand, really only too well aware of his son's character, nevertheless took refuge in his conception of Royal duty and indicated that he blamed Helen for the trouble more by what he failed to say than by what he actually said.

The Peasant Party insisted that she was an ally of the Bratianus who, through their financial affiliations in the Near East, could sell back the Greek throne to Helen's brother in the same way that they had once traded the crown of Rumania.

Carol, on his side, was steadily winning the political battle. Blood seemed to count, and the long lineage of rulers that was his ancestry had bestowed on him powers that automatically commanded admiration. His streak of restless individuality had combined with his traditional sense of princely behaviour with the result that he appealed both to the simple peasants, who were ready to accept the theory of the divine right of kings, and also to the post-war generation of the rapidly industrialising areas and the annexed territories where reform was the watchword.

He saw much that was wrong in the country. He did not hesitate to indicate that he disliked the corruption that gripped Rumania by the throat, and he did more than hint that in due time he would put many things right. His contributions to the welfare of the people were real. He had inspired a Boy Scout movement and was himself the Chief Scout of a quarter million strong membership. He had formed a great sports organisation and he was the pioneer of civil and military aviation.

He gained two nicknames at this time—Carol the Rapscallion and Carol the Bolshie. The amused admiration which is so often the human regard for a rake appealed to the Rumanian heart; the hope which his promises of reform aroused among the poor and deprived appealed to the Rumanian mind.

If, in effect, he held up a pair of scales to the Rumanian

(Right) Prince Carol of Rumania in 1902.

(Left) Carol's favourite portrait of himself as the "Warrior-King", the "First Peasant of Rumania", "Father of his People".

(Photo. Mansell Collection)

(*Left*) Carol's prospective bride: Grand Duchess Olga, eldest daughter of the last Tsar.

(Photo: Popper-Handke Collection

(*Right*) Princess Helen and her son Michael in 1925—at the time when her estrangement from Carol became an international topic and a Rumanian political crisis.

people, on one side the incubus of his private amours, and on the other his glittering promises of happier days, they did at least balance. And thousands of young Rumanians would have insisted that the good outweighed the bad.

At that time Carol could have ensured for himself both a secure throne and a secret mistress without real hindrance from anyone. His own foolish behaviour was in time to lose him the one, and his frantic efforts to regain it indicated that however great his desire for the red-haired beauty of Jassy, he did not entirely count the world well lost for love.

The situation could not endure, as Princess Helen had fervently told herself. In the early winter of 1925, Helena Lupescu presented herself at the police station at Jassy and stated that she wished to obtain a passport.

The local official told her to return next day when a decision would be forthcoming. She arrived, escorted by Carol. The Inspector, shuddering with fear that whatever he said would land him in trouble with his superiors, obsequiously invited the Crown Prince to take some refreshment while they discussed the matter.

Carol rather sullenly agreed. The official, who had sent his assistant rushing across to his house for his best glasses and for a bottle of vodka, began to dither and talk about the signs of a bad winter, the trials of his job and the lethargy of his superiors in Bucharest.

"It's not that I don't appreciate how busy they are there," he added hastily, recollecting that there were at least three highly placed officials at Bucharest police headquarters who seemed to prefer favourable reports on Madame Lupescu rather than the libellous ones that pleased their colleagues.

"Come to the point," growled the Prince. "Does Madame get her passport or doesn't she?"

The unfortunate man wrung his hands.

"It is a matter of the records, your Royal Highness,"

D

he explained apologetically. "Madame is, of course, well known in this town and is a highly respected citizen of Jassy. For myself, the passport would be an automatic procedure authorised with my wholehearted approval."

A policeman opportunely arrived with vodka and the glasses which gave the embarrassed Inspector a breathing space.

After they had gulped down their drinks he plunged again into an unwilling explanation.

"You must try to understand, Your Royal Highness, and you, Madame, that since the dissolution of your marriage the matter has become more complicated. You are registered at the address of your new house, but there is also the record that you have removed to Bucharest. The authorisation is therefore not solely my concern. The police in the capital have to countersign my approval."

"Does she get the passport?" the Prince repeated ominously.

"I am sure she will." The Inspector tried to make his tone sound convincing. "I am assured from Bucharest that the papers are on their way."

Carol rose and crossed to the telephone on the wall. "Get out!" he ordered peremptorily.

The Inspector hastily made himself scarce.

Twenty minutes later Carol opened the inner door. "You may issue the passport," he said graciously. "You have my word as your Crown Prince that you will not be exceeding your duty. Your job will not be jeopardised. In fact," he went on with that boyish smile that could in a trice transform the expression on his face from ill temper to irresistible charm, "it may in due course prove a great asset to your career."

The man's gratitude was pathetic. Intoxicated with this opportunity of ingratiating himself with his future King, he was bold enough to issue an invitation to luncheon.

"A modest meal, Sire," he continued, already regretting his impetuosity, "in fact only some ciorba, but my wife knows how to make it."

It was Helena who accepted.

"But it would be delightful," she said, in her husky, slow voice. "His Royal Highness loves my ciorba; we must see if your wife is a better cook than I."

Carol jokingly wagered that only a woman of the older generation could have the experience to get ciorba really right.

It was one of the incidents which endeared the Crown Prince to his people despite all his failings. He was a true Rumanian in his love of traditional Rumanian life, and he was a true prince in that he had the common touch.

They sat in the little wooden house of the police Inspector and enjoyed the steaming bowls of ciorba, made in the traditional way with game and sour cream, seasoned with lemon, and eaten with black bread.

Afterwards, with the passport formalities concluded and the Inspector's enthusiastic promise that he would personally see that the Ministry issued the necessary documents within two days, they set off for Bucharest.

It was perhaps Carol's sense of the mischievous that took him to the palace that night. As he suspected, the news of his telephone call from Jassy had been instantly reported to the King. His father was simple enough to feel relieved that his son's mistress wanted to leave the country. To him it meant that she was tired of Carol and would soon find another lover abroad.

Queen Marie, however, with a mind as subtle as her son's, saw real danger. She guessed that Carol had not underrated the ruthlessness of the Bratianus and had determined to get Helena out of harm's way. She suspected that once the woman was across the border, Carol might follow.

The Government saw eye to eye with the Queen, but they had complete faith in their ability to hold Carol prisoner. There had been no time to consult the palace when that angry, imperative voice had come over the wires from Jassy, and they had decided on the spot to accede to his wishes. Madame Lupescu could have her passport. The sooner she went the better, but there would be no approval whatever for Carol to go abroad either officially or privately.

To the consternation of both Government and Court, Helena made no move to leave. She got her passport and continued to live discreetly in either the house at Jassy or the apartment on the outskirts of Bucharest. The nation was puzzled. Everyone was at a loss to forecast the next development.

It came from an unexpected quarter and through an event which no one could have prophesied. On November 20th, Queen Alexandra died in England. The usual diplomatic condolences and invitation to the funeral were exchanged.

King Ferdinand, an authority on etiquette, correctly stated that, through family and State ties, Rumania would have to be represented by the Crown Prince. In vain did the Government insist that it was madness to let Carol out of their sight and in vain did they suggest that Queen Marie, as a close relative of the British Royal family, would be a better representative.

The King called for Carol, told him he would be sent to London, and formally asked his son for his word of honour that he would return before Christmas.

Very quietly the Prince replied: "I do not wish to go. This business seems to have been arranged without consulting me at all. But if I am compelled to go I will also be compelled to give you the promise for which you ask."

The King angrily dismissed him, turning to papers on his desk as was his usual method of evading argument with a son he could not understand.

Carol rushed out of the King's study and found, as he

had expected, Ion Bratianu awaiting the result of the interview in an adjoining office.

The ensuing argument brought servants tip-toeing to eavesdrop. The voices of the two men were raised in violent fury, and when Bratianu actually ordered the Prince to be ready to catch a special train within two hours, Carol stormed out of the room in order, as he said afterwards, to prevent himself punching the Minister in the face.

He was not ready within two hours, nor by the following morning. Spies reported that he had gone straight to Madame Lupescu and the lights had been on all night.

Queen Marie sent him a little note, couched in affectionate terms as from a mother to her child, begging him to come and see her. She was genuinely upset by the death of Queen Alexandra with whom she had been on terms of deep friendship for years. For the sake of her family, and irrespective of convention and diplomatic need, she asked Carol to go to the funeral. Carol appeared most amenable, and kissed her affectionately by way of reply.

. While Carol's train left via the Southern route so that his mother-in-law, who had been staying with her daughter, could travel with him part of the way, Helena quietly left her house, and after a series of purposeless journeys to throw the trailing police spies off the scent, she crossed the border into Hungary.

By the time Carol arrived in London there was a telegram awaiting him. It was unsigned and said simply: "Have arrived safely." It had been sent from Paris.

The Crown Prince was received in London with the deference due to a country with treaty and family ties with Great Britain. The photographers swarmed round him, and the press broke out into a rash of colourful revelations. These were mostly inspired by Rumanian agents who had accompanied the Prince and who gave their slanderous indiscretions just sufficient fact to sound authentic.

For the first time, Carol was able to learn how notorious he was outside his own country. Nevertheless he handled a difficult situation with dignity. He was easily the most handsome Royal mourner in the procession, and his uniform brought colour to that grey day of sadness as a well-loved Queen went to her rest.

Afterwards, it was true that he sought entertainment in the very gay night life of London of the mid-twenties. He drank a lot of champagne because he was accustomed to a bottle or so most evenings of his life. He was pleasant to the women who contrived an introduction to him, because he was always courteous to women and he never disguised his liking for their company.

But the stories of drunken roysterings which brought a reprimand from Buckingham Palace itself, of wanderings around the West End in search of feminine comfort, and all the other crude aspersions were quite untrue.

His stay in England was brief. On the day that he caught the boat train at Victoria, Helena booked a sleeping berth on the Rome Express, using an assumed name. Her subterfuge was useless. Rumanian agents were loitering nearby when she bought a ticket for Milan.

Carol stopped in Paris for a few hours to meet Zizi and see his son Mircea. The interview was stormy. His first wife had been ready to yield to a Princess but not to a mistress.

Helena and Carol alighted at Milan within a few hours of each other. Bratianu's men were already there, and the address of the apartment Carol had rented through a friend he met by arrangement in London had already been discovered before the lovers arrived.

The Crown Prince had no intention of indulging in a clandestine affair. He accompanied Helena openly to the most fashionable restaurants, went with her to the opera, and permitted the few gay night clubs of the place to advertise their presence. But he was greatly angered by the false accounts of his activities which appeared in the Press, and notably in Rumanian newspapers, which clearly indicated that they came from inspired sources in Bucharest.

On Christmas Eve he sat down and wrote three letters— one to the King, one to Princess Helen, and one to Ion Bratianu—briefly informing them that he did not intend to return to Rumania. It was significant that he did not write to his mother.

The receipt of the letters caused uproar. Princess Helen, facing at last the reality of a situation which was really of long standing, tearfully begged that she be permitted to go to Milan and persuade her husband to return, if not for her sake, then for the sake of their son. The King brusquely refused.

She went to see Bratianu. He was in conference with Prince Stirbey. They indicated to her that she should not interfere. Despite their outward appearance of sympathy, she had the impression that this was the moment they had been waiting for, when they could be rid of an irresponsible young man for ever.

To obviate any suggestion that they had given Carol an ultimatum the Bratianu faction agreed with the King that he should send the Marshal of the Court to Milan with a personal message.

The letter he bore was a futile mixture of peremptory command and a sentimental appeal.

Carol listened impatiently, and without taking any time for thought angrily told the Marshal: "You can inform my Father that I do not wish to be considered a member of the Royal Family. I consider that I have the right to bear another name to signify my severance with the Royal House of Rumania. In renouncing the throne verbally in the presence of Madame Lupescu and yourself, I confirm what I have already written. I will add a promise not to be the cause of strife or dissension in my

Father's kingdom by stating that I will not return to Rumania for ten years to come."

On the last day of 1925 the Crown Council met. To all intents and purposes the business was formal, with the King agreeing without comment to every proposal made by Ion Bratianu and Prince Stirbey. Had it not been for Ferdinand's anger against Carol he would have regarded as *lèse majesté* their insulting comments on his son's character.

On January 4th, 1926, the National Assembly was asked to approve a communique by the Crown Council.

It stated:

"His Royal Highness, Prince Carol, heir to the throne, having informed His Majesty in writing of his irrevocable renunciation of the succession to the Throne and all prerogatives appertaining to that rank, including that of membership of the Royal Family, His Majesty the King has deemed himself compelled to accept this renunciation and to summon a Council at the Castle of Pelesh. In communicating his high decision, His Majesty appealed to all men of eminence in the country who were present, to help him in its execution and in the proclamation of his grandson, Prince Michael as Heir to the Throne."

It was a clever piece of composition, thrusting all responsibility for proposing the decision on the King in person, and suggesting that there was all-party agreement on its execution.

In the clamour of approval from the Bratianu faction, the protests of the Peasant Party and the Transylvanian Nationalists were hardly heard. The renunciation was accepted.

On the first evening as a private person and as an exile, Carol remained at home with Helena, playing cards. He felt free for the first time in his life.

8

1926—1927

DURING the Spring of 1926, Carol put out his first feelers as to his father's reaction to a request for a divorce. He might have known that on both religious and State grounds, King Ferdinand would never consider such a step.

The request also horrified Princess Helen, and in a desperate hope that she might at least keep the façade of her marriage intact she again begged permission to try to see Carol in Italy and persuade him to reconsider his decision to desert her.

It may well have been that Carol hated his wife so deeply at this time that he deliberately tortured her by first of all saying that he would gladly meet her at any time she wished. Then, on the day that she was to take the train from Bucharest to Switzerland, she received a last-minute message in which Carol stated that he had changed his mind and had no intention of meeting her.

Without much doubt Helena Lupescu encouraged Carol to deny his arrangements in this way. Whenever the ex-Prince talked of letters or couriers from Rumania, she always pretended to shiver, commenting: "It brings the cold of the *crivat* whenever you mention that place."

The *crivat* was the bitterly cold north wind from the Russian steppes which always heralded the depth of winter.

Princess Helen went on her trip to Italy just the same to visit her grandmother. On her return to Bucharest she found that the King and Queen had been deeply upset by her failure to talk to Carol. It seemed that they recognised at last the inevitable end of the marriage.

Queen Marie, who could be extremely ruthless when she wished, had some idea of getting the Government to cut off Carol's emoluments. But the King, duly fearful of the still deeper troubles which might be caused if his son became a penniless exile and was tempted to write his memoirs for the fabulous sums which European and American press agencies were already offering him, insisted that they should be maintained.

"He is, after all, still a Prince," he said firmly.

It was perfectly true that Carol was fairly well off. His life was an expensive one, but despite all the slanderous stories that emanated from Italy, it was by no means a Saturnalia. He and Helena moved to Paris in the middle of the summer and took an apartment house in the suburb of Neuilly.

The proximity of her husband and his mistress was too much for Zizi Lambrino and she sued Carol in the French courts for the huge sum of ten million francs, alleging desertion. It seemed possible that it would be a protracted and notorious case, but in the preliminary hearing the judge found for Carol, insisting that the annulment of the marriage arranged by the High Court of Rumania was perfectly legal internationally. Not until February, 1957, nearly four years after Carol's death did this legal dispute reach its climax. Then the Portugese Supreme Tribunal of Justice declared Mircea Gregoire Lambrino the legitimate son of Carol.

Carol and Helena continued to enjoy life in Paris, mixing with the smart international set and being extremely well liked by a wide variety of friends and acquaintances, not least of them being the large number of Russian refugee aristocrats who had settled in the French capital. Despite the illicit nature of their liaison, Helena and Carol did, during these months, effectively quash the slanderous tales which had hitherto been told of their drinking parties, lavish gambling and generally unpleasant behaviour.

Queen Marie became genuinely alarmed that the world, already in two camps as regards the pros and cons of the battle of the Royal Family versus the Crown Prince, might transfer its sympathy entirely to Carol's side. It would be easy, she feared, to suggest that he was more sinned against than sinning, and that he had been virtually driven into the arms of Helena Lupescu by the coldness of his wife, married to him at the behest of his family.

With her usual brilliance the Queen decided to see if she could bring some of the limelight back to her side. With the help of wealthy ex-Rumanian business men who now resided in the United States, she secured an invitation to visit that country with Prince Nicolas and Princess Ileana. She set off and received a ticker-tape welcome in New York, thereafter making a spectacular tour of the United States and Canada. Not once in the hundreds of press interviews or at her meetings with women's clubs and civic notables, did she ever mention her wayward son.

The urgent necessity of this journey had been heightened by her knowledge that King Ferdinand was ill. Shortly before she arranged her visit to America, Queen Marie had been told by German doctors summoned to Bucharest that Ferdinand was suffering from early cancer which might or might not be operatable.

When she left, he was a sick man but not gravely ill. But the illness developed quickly. While Queen Marie was enjoying herself in the United States, the lonely old King had no one but the equally lonely Princess Helen to comfort him. She spent hours at his bedside, and the austere old man, who had refused to make a speech of welcome at his daughter-in-law's first official function in Rumania, now found a deep and comforting intimacy with her because, like himself, she knew what desolation and pain meant.

There was a tacit understanding between them not to mention Carol. Both were tortured by the knowledge that they wanted to love him, and did still love him despite his unworthiness.

By November, the King was so seriously ill that Queen Marie was summoned back. She cut short her United States visit and sailed in the *Berengaria* at the end of the month. Early in 1927 he underwent an operation which was regarded as successful and Queen Marie proposed to take him for convalescence to Sicily. He was, however, too weak to be moved and until May he could not even be taken from the Cotroceni Palace. Sensing that his life was nearing its end, he insisted that he be moved to Scroviste Peris.

It was not only the place where he had been able to enjoy the life of a Commanding General of the Rumanian armies, but there was also his hunting box from which he could look out over the rolling countryside and feel far removed from the unhappy worries of Bucharest.

He was by now so ill that the summer-time heat exhausted him seriously and his doctors told Queen Marie that the only chance to combat his increasing weakness would be to get him into the mountain air.

The change proved a fatal one. The cold of the nights at a high altitude gave the King a chill which quickly turned to pneumonia. For several days and nights while the disease slowly destroyed him, Queen Marie never left the bedside.

In the last hours before he died on July 27th, 1927, Ferdinand referred to his son.

"Carol," he said weakly, "he is a good boy really—very clever." Then with an uncharacteristic attempt at humour he added: "He is like a Swiss cheese, excellent for what it is but so very full of holes."

Carol had been informed of his father's serious illness and also that he was likely to die quite suddenly. He made no attempt to communicate with his parents and the announcement of the King's death left him quite un-moved.

"It is not that my love for him has died because of his attitude over my personal life," he said to a friend. "It is rather that I have never had any affection for him, nor he for me."

The charge that King Ferdinand had not loved his son was unfair and also untrue. Only a few days before his death the King gave instructions to an old general whom he could trust absolutely to visit the Prince and convey to him a message.

This said: "There remains only one course for Prince Carol and that is to be consistent with himself in the life which, against the desires of all, he has determined to create for himself, and to respect loyally and without reservation the inexorable consequences of his renunciation of the throne. Any agitation made in his name or even without his consent would tend to compromise the interests of the dynasty."

The King's forebodings that there might be trouble after his death were only too justified. For many weeks the amount of political intrigue had increased greatly and there was a strong movement to bring Carol back secretly to Rumania and present a *fait accompli* to the nation as soon as the announcement of the death of the reigning monarch should be made.

Secret police reports stated that there was a strong movement in the provinces to create civil disturbances if it should be announced that the infant Michael was regarded as the next King. The Government could, however, work fast and so effectively prevent the other side doing very much.

The announcement of Michael as King of Greater Rumania was made in less than an hour after King Ferdinand's death, and at the same time the names of the members of the Regency which would rule for him were given. They were three in number—Prince Nicolas, the Patriarch, and the President of the Court of Cassation. The Government was too contemptuous of Princess

Helen and too wary of Queen Marie to include them.

These three men were really nothing but stooges for the Bratianus. They had no legal power and less initiative. The new boy King, who was still under six years of age, was taken to the Cathedral, and then to Parliament House on the following day, to watch the religious and civic ceremonies when the Regents took their oath of allegiance. He spent most of his time in church examining a cut on his knee.

Many patriotic Rumanians, irrespective of their feelings towards Prince Carol, were disgusted and alarmed at the machinations of the Bratianu interests in arranging the Regency as they had.

Within a few days there emerged a People's Party which was blatantly in favour of bringing Carol back and proclaiming him King, whether he gave up Helena Lupescu or not. The Government arrested one of the leaders of this party on charges of carrying letters from Carol to traitors in Bucharest. At his trial, to the fury of the Government, he was acquitted and was carried out shoulder high from the court.

On the following Sunday several thousand peasants marched on an organised plan to make a demonstration in Bucharest. The weather turned out very bad, and the march took many of the peasants far longer than they had expected. The whole thing became rather comic when the organisers had to apply to the Government for transport facilities to get them back.

For a time, therefore, the Bratianus had the situation completely under control, but in November, 1927, Ion Bratianu died. His brother, Vintila, became Prime Minister, but although he bore such a famous name, he was a man of little character.

Meantime, Carol and Helena moved into a new house in the outskirts of Paris—a much more modest establishment. The grants of money were arriving irregularly and the Prince was compelled to economise. Some of his servants were dismissed and then he had to get rid of others who, he found out, were spies working for the Rumanian Government. He became disheartened and depressed.

Helena and he quite often quarrelled and neighbours told with some truth of the shouting and hysterical screaming that they could hear at night. Helena's chief complaint was that Carol had too weak a character. "You must be a man" she insisted, and she scolded him for putting off everything until the morrow.

Their life was now far removed from all the slanderous stories which were told in Rumania of their hectic and dissipated amusements—of their gambling with vast sums of money every night and drinking with their cronies.

In fact, at this period Helena was doing the cooking— an activity which she loved, while Carol actually had to do some of the house-cleaning and make the bed—an occupation which was certainly most distasteful to him.

There was probably no ulterior motive whatever in Carol's decision to write to Princess Helen, or as she was now known, the Queen Mother, and once again ask for a divorce. It was nothing to do with any desire to return to Rumania, but was simply that he wanted above all to marry Helena and bring some security into his life. In their quarrels she was always threatening to leave him.

Carol's letter begged his wife in most urgent terms to reconsider her previous decision never to agree to a divorce and pointed out that the promise she had given to King Ferdinand, who, as a Catholic, could never have agreed to the dissolution of his son's marriage, was not now binding.

Helen showed the letter to the Prime Minister and also to the principal members of the opposition parties. For once they were in agreement. None of them wanted a divorce to be granted.

The Bratianus rejected the proposal because they realised how greatly it would strengthen Carol's claim to return if he ever desired to put it to the Rumanian people. The Peasant Party, although they would have done almost anything to further their plan to bring the Prince back, nevertheless had to take into account the strong religious attitude of their members, and they knew that Madame Lupescu would not be accepted by them even as the morganatic wife of their King while his real wife lived.

In a cold and formal communication, written in the third person, Helen informed her husband that she could not accede to his request.

The application had one beneficial result for Carol. His financial matters were eased by a more regular despatch of his allowance. Helena and he moved to the French Riviera and became one of the best known couples at Nice, the centre of attention in the casino, and well known to tourists when they took their regular morning stroll along the Promenade des Anglais.

Sometimes Helena did not accompany the Prince on his more energetic walks, and whenever she was absent, he was always hunted by a bevy of women of great beauty but doubtful morals. Many of these had been planted in Carol's hotel and had been ordered by the Bratianu faction to do their best to compromise him. It said much for his discretion that he always managed diplomatially to get out of the innumerable awkward situations in which these women tried to corner him.

In Rumania the situation was also ostensibly quite placid. But unknown even to the secret police at first, a new figure began slowly to come into prominence. He was Barbu Ionescu. This deceptively quiet and bored-looking man was in fact one of the most enterprising Rumanians of the many who had moved beyond the borders of the kingdom in the first twenty years of the century and became rich and powerful in other countries.

Ionescu had at one time been a waiter in a small London restaurant. From that lowly beginning he started in the coffee business, and with various other trades connected with catering he amassed a large income just before and during the first World War. He was well known in business circles in London, Paris and Brussels.

By 1927, when he became the closest friend that Prince Carol had, he was one of the richest men in Western Europe. It was Ionescu who smuggled into Rumania signed statements by Carol that, while he was making no personal plans to return to the country, he would not be deaf to any request from the mass of the people to come back and ascend the throne. Ionescu found such a favourable reaction to these letters that he suggested to Carol that he should come with Madame Lupescu to England.

They stayed at Ionescu's home—Oakhurst Court, Godstone, Surrey. Every effort had been made to keep the visit private, but, unfortunately, Carol insisted on going to the West End of London during his stay. A visit to a London theatre was arranged and the management let it be known to the press that Carol and his Titian-haired mistress were to be among the audience.

As a result, there was an enormous crowd outside the theatre entrance, and when Helena Lupescu stepped from her host's car, women rushed at her from all sides. Helena was terrified and started to cry hysterically. Carol rushed forward to protect her, lost his temper and struck out at some of the people who were trying to touch her. The crowd grabbed souvenirs. Helena was wearing a short mink coat and they pulled out large tufts of fur before she reached the shelter of the foyer.

The next morning they received a visit from an emissary from Buckingham Palace, who suggested that this sort of publicity did no one any good, and requested Carol to behave more discreetly in the future, keeping out of London whenever possible.

Meantime, the British Foreign Office was investigating the reason for Carol's visit. What they discovered alarmed them.

One morning, just before luncheon, a Scotland Yard Detective Inspector arrived at Oakhurst Court and requested to see the Prince.

"I have to convey to you, sir, a decision of the Home Office," the officer began, "that you are requested to leave Great Britain as soon as possible."

Carol's face went white, and in a shaking voice, barely concealing his temper, he replied: "This is terribly painful; may I ask the reason?"

"I can give your Royal Highness no reason," replied the police officer.

He then went on to explain that the British Government considered it desirable, both in the interests of Rumania and of Great Britain, that Prince Carol should leave as soon as reasonably possible. It was hinted that the time limit would be forty-eight hours.

Immediately after the Inspector left, Prince Carol went in Ionescu's car to Scotland Yard where he again demanded to know the reason for the expulsion order. A suave member of the Special Branch to which this delicate matter of expelling a Prince of Royal blood had been entrusted, refused to give any further explanation. Carol made no further comment and left immediately.

The interest of the British Government in Carol's activities in England had resulted from alarming reports received through the Secret Service and also from the Rumanian Government.

Reliable information was forthcoming that powerful political groups connected with the minor officials of the Peasant Party were arranging for a series of demonstrations in all the main provincial cities, in favour of Prince Carol's ascent to the throne. At these rallies, involving many hundreds of thousands of people, it was rumoured that some sort of manifesto would be forthcoming in which Carol would promise to rectify all the nation's wrongs as soon as he was proclaimed King.

The most rigorous investigation by the Rumanian

police had failed to unearth any printing plant which was preparing this document. There was, however, a reliable story that copies would arrive from a foreign country.

While the Foreign Office and the Special Branch were in conference as to how Carol's living in England could be involved in this matter, a message came from the Traffic Controller at Croydon Airport—at that time the main air station for London—in which he requested that permission be obtained for an international flight beyond France.

This was an unusually long air journey for those days and immediately more detailed investigation of the passengers and the purpose of the trip was started.

The order proved to be for two aircraft, one of which was to carry freight and the other three passengers. The aircraft were to land at Le Bourget, refuel, and then resume their journey for an unspecified destination beyond Austria.

Matters developed rapidly that day. Queen Marie sent a personal message to Buckingham Palace requesting that the rumoured flight of her son and his mistress should be prevented at all costs.

Further Secret Service reports indicated that one of the aircraft was to scatter leaflets over the peasant rallies and that the second would, a short time afterwards, land at Jassy.

From this machine, Prince Carol was to step in the uniform of an officer of the Rumanian Air Force and was then to lead the peasants in a triumphal procession to the capital, where he would be proclaimed King.

The French police authorities were able to report that several million leaflets in the Rumanian language were already being printed in Paris. They were, however, powerless to prevent their distribution as they had received no official request from Rumania.

The situation was regarded as so serious that there was a Cabinet meeting at which the order was given to

Scotland Yard to interview Carol and tell-him that he must leave the country by ship. At the same time, Croydon Airport received an order to ground the two aircraft which had, in fact, been commissioned by Ionescu for the trip.

Men of the Special Branch made a hurried search for Carol's whereabouts that evening. It was believed that a private room booked at a London hotel in the name of Captain Mesurier—a name which Prince Carol had quite often used when he resided incognito in hotels on the French Riviera—was to be the scene of the final conference between Carol, Helena Lupescu and Ionescu.

Detectives waited in the hotel until past midnight, but apparently a Rumanian waiter had got wind of what was going on and had let Ionescu know that it would be inadvisable for the dinner to take place. The next morning the Detective Inspector went to Godstone where the ultimatum was given.

After Carol's unsatisfactory interview at Scotland Yard he returned to Godstone and then again left for London. He was smiling and pleasant but refused any statement to the reporters who had rushed down from London and were crowded round the gates of the house. During the late afternoon, Helena Lupescu, accompanied by Madame Ionescu and her children, drove by car to London. That evening, Carol and Helena took the ferry to France and after a brief stay in Paris went to live in Belgium.

On the evening of Carol's expulsion, Ionescu gave a press interview at which he said: "The Prince is staggered, surprised and shamed. We had thought such a thing was impossible in England. Here, we had thought to have a refuge from persecution and from jealousy. Yet this happened. I am more overwhelmed than I can say. What has the Prince done? He has simply tried to do his best for his country. The peasants are marching on his capital. He has wanted to avoid bloodshed. That is why he has issued his manifesto. What is there wrong in that?"

The crocodile tears of Ionescu over the cold-heartedness of the English authorities were a little hard to accept when it was realised that he was greatly exaggerating the position. No peasants were marching on the capital because no Prince had descended from the skies to lead them. No manifesto had been issued because the aircraft to take it had been grounded at Croydon.

In Belgium, where Carol and Helena were guests in another house of Ionescu's, the set-back to the plans bitterly disappointed the Prince and aroused the fury of Helena. There were times when she taunted Carol for weakness and there were others when she said: "The British kicked you out, not me."

There was, however, plenty of tenacity in Carol's make-up and he was soon plotting once again to return to his country as King.

9

I F the factions which supported Princess Helen and her son King Michael thought that Carol's behaviour during the Godstone incident had ruined his chances of regaining the throne, they were soon proved wrong. Ionescu was prepared to sink most of his fortune in engineering the restoration of Carol, and in fact before he succeeded he spent more than half a million sterling.

It was at Ionescu's instigation that Carol, as soon as he was settled in Belgium, sent to Princess Helen more and more urgent requests for a divorce.

His insistence embarrassed the members of the Peasant Party who were anxious to bring him back, because the continued existence of his marriage effectively prevented any possibility of his marrying Helena Lupescu. To many of the elderly and rural members this was the only safeguard they had against a Queen they would detest.

There were, however, other politicians who agreed with Carol that the interests opposing them were largely centred in Princess Helen, and however weak her personal political force might be, her status as Carol's wife would always be troublesome to them. For this reason they were anxious that the divorce should go through, and considerable pressure was brought to bear on Princess Helen to agree.

The unfortunate and lonely young woman was also assailed from a new and unexpected quarter. For some time Queen Marie had grown more and more hostile to her, the reason being jealousy over the upbringing of young King Michael.

Queen Marie was also strongly influenced by an intimate woman friend, an American dancer Loie Fuller. The friendship had begun more than twenty years before when Marie was a rather desperate and unhappy Princess trying to overcome her boredom in the Court of King Carol I.

Miss Fuller had been touring the capitals of Europe with her new form of dancing. She had conceived the idea of depicting emotions with the aid of coloured lights playing on the folds of the transparent chiffon gowns which she wore for her dances.

Princess Marie, accustomed to the rigid formality of classical ballet, was intrigued by Miss Fuller's performance and arranged to meet her afterwards. A deep friendship sprang up between them which lasted until Miss Fuller's death.

The American dancer, who, on her retirement, went to live in Paris, was probably the only person in the world who knew the truth about Queen Marie's personal life. There was never a week in the whole of the twenty odd years of their friendship that letters did not pass between them.

Loie Fuller knew about the hell of Queen Marie's married life; she knew how King Ferdinand had refused to show any affection for his son Carol; she knew of Queen Marie's increasing search for love and friendship among other men.

When Queen Marie made her American tour in 1926, the dancer, despite the fact that she was old and partially paralysed, made the journey to America so that they could meet.

It was then that Loie Fuller told Queen Marie that she had met Madame Lupescu in Paris and that she both liked and admired her. She had some critical and cruel things to say about Princess Helen, and the whole weight of her argument was on the side of the Prince and his mistress. She had a very real affection for Carol and she would have done anything to further his interest.

In her New York hotel the dancer, a wizened little

woman, sat up in bed and said with brutal frankness: "One day, Marie, and not so very long now, you may be as old and as helpless as I am. When that happens I pray you are not alone. I hope that you have a son who is a King and who can protect you."

Although Loie Fuller had the typical American attitude to divorce and the typical Republican's romantic feelings about marriage between a person of Royal blood and a commoner, she could see that Helena Lupescu might be a serious obstacle. If it had not been for Queen Marie's enforced return to the bedside of her dying husband, Miss Fuller's plans to provide Helena Lupescu with a large estate on which to live, financed by American sympathisers, would have come to fruition.

Now it was too late for that. When she read the letters from Queen Marie complaining about the coldness of her daughter-in-law and her unhappiness in being prevented from seeing or having any control over the education of Michael, she wrote back advising the Queen to throw all her influence on the side of Carol's restoration, even with his mistress by his side.

Soon afterwards, Loie Fuller wrote to Ionescu and suggested that he should persuade Carol to return to Paris where she could keep an eye on him and assist in any plans that might be made for a return to Rumania.

The campaign to force Princess Helen to agree to a divorce was intensified. There was nothing that her ruthless opponents would not do. The foulest of rumours had spread like wild-fire through Rumania, revealing quite untrue details of the Princess's sex life and indicating that Carol, far from being a guilty rapscallion, had in fact been a patient martyr.

The aspersions against Helen's womanhood and against her character quickly became so disgusting that she was driven from her resolve to accept anything rather than a divorce. In tears she went to Ion Bratianu and begged him to protect her reputation. But, for once, the wily

Prime Minister was powerless and he had to admit there was little he could do.

As anxious as he was to prevent any development which would facilitate Carol's return, he recognised that the mud being thrown at Princess Helen was already affecting her son. There was a very real danger that, whether Carol came back or not, Michael would be dethroned.

"While I am alive," Bratianu boasted, "I will see to it that Carol does not return, but my advice is for you to grant him the divorce he wants." But now Ion Bratianu was dead, and his brother Vintila made no such promise.

At a hurried and secretive session of the Rumanian Supreme Court on June 21st, 1928, the marriage was dissolved. Although the Carol faction had hoped to be able to give perjured evidence reflecting on Princess Helen, the authorities managed to make the hearing a mere formality and the grounds for the divorce were given as incompatibility.

In Paris, Carol and Helena Lupescu celebrated the news with a small dinner party. It was attended by Ionescu and several members of the Rumanian Peasant Party. Helena played her usual excellent role as the perfect hostess and she had the wisdom to behave with extreme discretion. As a result, one of the older guests, a man from the North of Rumania who had gone to criticise, left a devoted admirer.

He told his friends on his return: "Helena is neither a siren nor a vampire, but a charming and beautiful woman. I felt great sympathy for her because love had been so cruel. When she said to me: 'I have suffered; God, how I have suffered!' I felt my eyes fill with tears."

The breaking down of any misgivings of those who were politically favourable to Carol's restoration continued during the next few months. The ex-Crown Prince and his mistress lived very quietly. They kept to their house outside Paris and very rarely were seen in the night-clubs or gay restaurants of the French capital. Events soon furthered their campaign.

The world depression was starting and there were serious economic troubles in Rumania. Without the genius of Ion Bratianu, the Liberal Government which had ruled Rumania for so long saw its last days. The Regency, having failed to indicate that it could govern with any authority or wisdom, panicked and begged Maniu to form a Government. So at last the National Peasant Party came to power.

Within a few days of Maniu taking office he went to see Queen Marie and spoke with the uttermost frankness:

"I have always been against Prince Carol's retirement," he told her. "I have been against it not only because I do not think it would satisfy public opinion, but also because my dearest wish is to ensure the unblemished continuity of the dynastic order. In my capacity as Prime Minister I definitely favour the return of the Prince— but only under certain well-defined conditions."

These conditions, with Queen Marie's approval, he submitted to Carol in Paris. They were first, that he should submit to Parliamentary control, secondly that Madame Lupescu should not come back to Rumania.

Maniu had been worried about the latter stipulation because all his information was that Carol would angrily reject it. To his amazement his courier returned to Bucharest saying that the Prince had agreed instantly. More surprising still, Helena, who had been present at the interview, had said that she also was perfectly agreeable to this arrangement.

Maniu could not know why Helena had adopted this attitude. The reason was that she had been so deeply insulted a few days earlier that at the moment she loathed the very idea of ever entering her country again.

The proprietor of one of the newspapers supporting the National Peasant Party, a man named Seicaru, had visited Carol in Paris to discuss the future press campaign.

"The people love you," he said, "but with Madame at your side your chances of being anything more than a member of the Regency advising your son, the King, are very remote."

With a burst of violent and uncontrollable temper of the intensity which was later to gain so many enemies for him, Carol said that Helena was as good as any woman in Bucharest.

"It is impossible to make a flag out of a dirty rag, Sire," the newspaper proprietor retorted.

Helena had been listening to the interview behind an open door leading to an adjoining room. She rushed in and told Seicaru angrily that she would never set foot in a country which bred men who could utter such a contemptuous phrase.

She moved across to Carol and kissed him lightly on the forehead.

"My enemies are mean enough to pretend that I am a wicked woman," she said. "What I am going to do now will doubtless influence them to say that I am also a woman scorned. I do not mind. The choice is entirely mine. I renounce our perfect love."

Carol stood up and put his arm around her, telling the newspaper proprietor to get out. When they were alone he said how proud he was of her gesture in making such a sacrifice.

"You know the old Rumanian proverb," he went on, " 'If you are the anvil, suffer; if the hammer, strike.' At the moment you are the anvil, my darling, but the day is not far away when I shall be the hammer."

She smiled.

"I understand," she answered. "There is another Rumanian proverb which says 'Kiss the hand you cannot bite.' "

Carol nodded.

"At the moment I have to accept the unpleasant suggestions of these peculiar people who are being useful to me. You need have no fear. I have said that I have no intention of living without you, and I repeat it now. What will a few days, a few weeks matter compared with a life-time when I am King?"

The months dragged past. In Rumania the rosy promises of the new Government proved false. The nation was in a bad way. More and more people began to believe that Carol's return would produce some magical cure for the economic illness of Rumania.

On the first day of June, 1930, Carol and Helena made a well-publicised trip to Switzerland. Most of the newspapers in France, England, and the United States reported that they were going for a holiday. The parting came at Berne after they had dined in a small restaurant.

Helena went by car to a villa at Vitznau which Carol had rented for her. He had got to know the place during his stay at Lucerne when he became engaged to Princess Helen. It was a delightful little village at the foot of the Rigi, well away from the public eye, about half a dozen miles from Lucerne.

Carol drove next morning to Paris and on June 7th, under the name of Captain Mesurier, entered a small plane at Le Bourget airport. The aircraft flew to Munich and then went on through the short summer's night.

The people of Rumania were left under no illusions about the alleged holiday in Switzerland. In every town and village the report spread that Carol was coming back. With brilliant cleverness the Government kept the details vague. But in order to attract crowds and to increase the atmosphere of expectations, special preparations were made at airports all over the country with troops in full ceremonial dress on parade all Saturday evening.

Carol landed at 8 o'clock on the Sunday morning at Baneasa airfield outside Bucharest, where he was met by Prince Nicolas, representing the Regency, and by the chief Ministers of the Government. It was a brilliant sunny morning and the scene was magnificently staged. Carol stepped from the aircraft in Air Force uniform, looking handsome, tall, still lean, and every inch a King.

The thousands of people who had trooped out of Bucharest the previous evening and had slept through the hot summer's night on the perimeter of the airfield, did not cheer him as he walked towards the waiting carriage. Instead they knelt in the dust beside the road as if worshipping him as a god who had descended from the skies.

The procession into Bucharest was a triumph every mile of the way. The streets were decorated and hung with flags. Before Carol reached the Government buildings, the interior of his carriage was half buried in flowers. The morning was entirely his.

Princess Helen had not even been informed of Carol's arrival, and nobody went to tell her until some hours after he had arrived in Bucharest.

Queen Marie knew all about the project, but she was staying in her villa at Balcic, on the coast of the Black Sea. She was wise enough to know that all this jubilation was ephemeral, and Carol would need every bit of support that could be given to him. She had no intention of detracting from it by being present herself on this historic morning.

Inside the Government buildings, Carol refused to confer with the Regency and the Cabinet until he had made a telephone call. There was a delay in putting him through to Switzerland but in half an hour he heard Helena's anxious voice come thinly and faintly over the line.

"Have you succeeded?"

"Yes," he answered. "I am here but I am already feeling the desperate loneliness of being without you."

"You had to go," she said. "But now that you are back in Bucharest I am afraid that you will forget me."

"I swear I never will do that," he vowed.

During the remainder of the day, Carol had a series of stormy interviews with his Ministers and with members of the Regency. The general idea had been that he would for a time at least become a member of the Regency, probably in place of his brother Nicolas. A Government announcement would then be made that the procedure was being considered for making him King, so that the people could accustom themselves to the idea of the change.

Carol rejected this proposal outright and said that in his own estimation he was already King of Rumania in fact, if not by ritual.

Maniu tried to temporise by suggesting that all the other members of the Regency should resign and that Carol should for the time being become a sort of King Father. This proposal was also immediately rejected by Carol, but he agreed to await the decision of the National Assembly of the Peasant Party before making any public announcement.

His dictatorial attitude alarmed the Government. When he left for the Cotroceni Palace to take dinner with his brother Nicolas, a discreet order was issued to the Chief of Police to keep him under constant supervision.

At some time during the night the Bucharest Police Chief, General Nicoleanu, received orders from the Government actually to arrest Carol and hold him *incommunicado*. Nicoleanu made a gesture of obeying orders by sending squads of men to the night clubs and cafés of the capital to look for him. They had instructions to make no attempt, however, to enter the Palace where, of course, everybody knew that Carol was resting.

Carol and Nicolas sat up far into the night discussing the situation. An amazing decision resulted.

Nicolas told Carol of the considerable popularity of the young King for reasons of sentiment towards a child. He suggested that the most effective way to counteract any opposition from the quarters favourable to Michael and through him to his mother, Helen, would be to have the divorce annulled.

Carol had little hesitation in agreeing to this proposal, although, as he commented, he had no intention of resuming marital relations with his wife.

On the following morning, Carol got in touch with his sister Elizabetta and asked her to go and see Helen to tell her that he intended to send for King Michael during the day. Helen had to tell her eight-year-old son that his father had recovered from a long illness and had returned unexpectedly to Bucharest in an aeroplane.

She warned the child, who was already very conscious of the fact that he was a King, that it was unusual for little boys to reign over a country and that his father would probably take over the duty until he was old enough to rule himself. The summons from Carol for Michael did not, however, arrive that day.

At mid-morning, the Cabinet met to consider Carol's proposals. Six members were in favour of his being proclaimed King immediately, and five insisted that for the time being he should be a member of the Regency. Maniu himself was among the latter.

As the Cabinet was so nearly split, it was agreed that the question should be submitted to all members of the National Peasant Party. Delegates representing every group in the country were awaiting the outcome of the Cabinet conference, and when they were requested to vote on the matter, it was found that they were overwhelmingly in favour of Carol being proclaimed King immediately.

Maniu went to see Carol, who was impatiently pacing up and down in an adjoining room. He informed him of the Cabinet's decision and added a personal request. This required Carol to state categorically that he had no intention of bringing Helena Lupescu back to Rumania.

Carol angrily refused to be dictated to by a commoner, even if he happened to be his Prime Minister, and the old man quietly offered his resignation. Immediately Carol, who had a remarkable talent for persuasion, begged Maniu to reconsider his decision. He pointed out that Helena Lupescu was not in the country; also that she herself had said in the presence of the Rumanian delegate that she was giving him up for ever.

Carol watching the Prime Minister closely, saw that he had gained his point. With real humility, Maniu thanked Prince Carol for his confidence and said that he would like to withdraw his offer of resignation.

"Splendid!" exclaimed Carol, all his gaiety returning. "Now all that remains is to make the public ceremony of my accession to the throne."

, That afternoon he drove in a horse-drawn open carriage to the Parliament buildings amid excited, cheering crowds. Without any opposition the Act of January 4th, 1926, was declared invalid and Carol II was proclaimed King. It was also stated that it would be assumed that he had automatically become King at the moment of the death of his father, King Ferdinand.

This peculiar procedure of attempting to re-write history and abolish the very fact that young King Michael had ever sat on the throne, was the final bitterness of that day to Princess Helen. She was numbed with misery, and when Prince Nicolas arrived shortly after the nation-wide broadcast of the proceedings in Parliament had finished, she refused to hand over her son so that he should be taken to Carol at the Cotroceni Palace.

Prince Nicolas warned her that if she persisted in her refusal, it certainly would not enhance the future welfare of either herself or of Michael. Helen, however, had resolved to fight for the only thing she still possessed, her son's affection, and she refused to consider anything but a personal interview with Carol.

Rather to everybody's surprise, Carol made no objections, and early that evening he arrived at the house where Helen was living. He entered the main hall in company with his brother Nicolas and his sister Elizabetta. Princess Helen noted that he had hardly changed at all in the five years since she had last seen him. Indeed he looked wonderfully well and quite boyish, despite his 37 years. She realised at the same time that unhappiness had not dealt so kindly with her.

Carol started to go up the stairs two at a time to the large landing where he could see Princess Helen was standing. Suddenly he paused. He had seen that behind her was her aide-de-camp holding Michael by the hand.

Acutely sensitive to any slight to himself, Carol was remarkably obtuse when it came to understanding how other people could suffer, and he had blithely expected the meeting with his ex-wife to be a homely, informal affair.

His face darkened with anger when he saw that this was to be a ceremony before witnesses. After a moment, however, he recovered and continued up the stairs. He tried to kiss Helen but she drew back and offered him her hand. Her coldness at that moment, however understandable, destroyed for ever any remote chance of salvaging the wreckage of their marriage.

Carol shook her hand, smiled and said: "Hello."

Helen did not reply for several seconds and they stared at one another in silence. Finally, she said: "The only thing for us to do is to be friends for Michael's sake."

"I quite agree," Carol answered. "We will not talk of the past. All I have come for is to see Michael."

Helen motioned to the aide-de-camp to leave them, and taking the boy by the hand, led the way into a drawing-room. Once inside, Carol drew Michael to him and kissed him over and over again. The child, who hardly remembered his father, began to whimper. With pleading eyes he turned to his mother and said: "I do not want Papa to take me away."

"Of course he won't," Helen answered, looking at

E

Carol meaningly. "You are only going to the Palace to have a little chat with him."

Carol asked Helen if she would have a few minutes' private conversation with him as he had some extremely personal matters to discuss. Helen blankly refused to agree to this, whereupon the King said that there was no point in continuing the discussion any further, and that he would take his son to the Palace.

"Public opinion demands that Michael be seen with me," he pointed out. "But I shall not keep him long, as I realise it is near his bed-time. Elizabetta will bring him back within an hour."

Carol and Michael drove into Bucharest and an enormous crowd greeted them delightedly when Carol led his son on to a balcony of the Palace. Afterwards Michael was taken to the Palace every day, but Helen never accompanied him. The periods that he was with his father became longer and longer.

Politically everything seemed to be running smoothly and Maniu, whose qualms about Carol's behaviour had been entirely abolished by the excellent way in which he conducted himself, began to talk about the Coronation. He told Carol that it was essential that Helen should be crowned Queen at the same time. Carol made no objection to this, adding that it was the Government's job to see, as he expressed it, "that the formalities are ostentatiously observed."

Carol pretended to his Ministers that he had no objection whatsoever to an ostensible reconciliation. In fact, he inferred that he desired it, doubting only that anyone could persuade Princess Helen to agree.

The Princess, not unnaturally, refused point-blank to make the first move.

A series of deputations by members of the Government introduced the suggestion which Carol so adroitly put into their minds. Ruthlessly and steadily they wore Helen down until through sheer desperation she said that she would agree to an annulment of the divorce, provided there were certain provisions regarding the resumption of her married life with Carol. These were of such an intimate nature that they could be discussed only with the King himself.

A tiny spark of hope was born in her breast after she had said this, a spark which tempted her to believe that after all, Carol might still have some affection for her, and that he was feeling some remorse for the happenings of the past few years.

This hope was cruelly extinguished when Prince Nicolas arrived with a personal message from Carol in which he asked her to write him a letter formally requesting that the divorce should not be annulled.

"In spite of all that you have been told by his Ministers," Nicolas said, "I can assure you that your ex-husband is to-day even more strongly against an annulment of your divorce than you have ever been. But you see the predicament he is in! The public is clamouring for a reconciliation and the only solution for him is for you to appear as the one who objects."

Helen, subdued and brow-beaten, took the pen which was thrust into her hand by Nicolas. But as she sat down to write, she had an idea of how to phrase her letter so that it would suggest to any third party that it had been written under duress.

Carol was furious when he read the letter because he realised that it would be impossible to issue it to the press. A few days later he arrived unannounced at Helen's house just before luncheon. She was forced to invite him to stay for a meal at which neither spoke one word.

Afterwards, when the servants had been dismissed, he talked to her quite naturally of his plans for the future of Rumania. Under the mellowing influence of what had been a very good meal and the considerable amount of wine which he drank at it, he became quite kindly and confessed to her that there had been much to blame on both sides. He told her that, in his opinion, the marriage had always been unwise because their characters were so different.

When Carol realised that he had at last persuaded Helen to consider the situation without anger, he again returned to the subject of the annulment of their divorce. He repeated all the arguments that Nicolas had used as to the desirability of her spontaneously insisting that she did not want an annulment.

"I know the people desire that there should be a reconciliation between us," he said, "but I am not in a position to satisfy their wish."

Helen told him that she had no intention of going any further than she had done already in the letter that she had written him. Although Carol refrained from any direct rudeness at not getting his own way, he became cold and taciturn, and left without expressing any opinion as to what he would do.

After he had gone, Helen sat quietly thinking. The strange way in which Carol had stressed the importance of his not making any move about the reconciliation, no matter how superficial, renewed in her mind a rumour that had come to her ears—a rumour that was already talked about throughout Rumania.

It was said that shortly after Carol and Helena Lupescu had arrived in Belgium they had been secretly married. This rumour was not one that convinced Maniu. He believed that time would heal the breach between the King and Helen and that the Coronation which was due to be held in the latter half of September, would solve all the problems.

He made detailed arrangements during the last weeks of July for the ceremony, actually issuing contracts for the decorations, the construction of the procession stands, and discussing with the Patriarch the position of the twin thrones in the Cathedral where Carol and

Helen would be crowned King and Queen of Greater
Rumania.

So convinced was he that everything was running
smoothly that at the beginning of August he took two
weeks' holiday. It was a time when everybody who could
get out of Bucharest did so. Princess Helen herself left to
escape the heat and stayed at Pelesh Castle.

While she was away, Carol sent servants to her home
to remove various pieces of furniture—those which he had
ordered from London—and a considerable proportion
of the stock in the wine cellar. They were taken to the
Foishor where Carol and his brother Nicolas had gone.

It was noted that a large proportion of the servants
at the Foishor had either been dismissed or transferred to
other Royal residences and that several foreign-looking
servants had arrived to replace them.

The usual and inevitable rumours about Carol's
amatory activities began to spread. But no one for a time
hit on the identity of the woman who had been so discreetly installed at the Foishor. The heads of the
Rumanian Secret Police who were responsible personally
to the Prime Minister and not to the King, were quite
certain that the woman who was occasionally seen at the
windows of the Palace was some local beauty from
Bucharest.

Ever since Carol had returned, every road and every
railway station on Rumanian frontiers had been staffed
by special men from Bucharest police headquarters,
briefed with all possible details of Helena Lupescu.
They reported daily that there was no sign of her.

It may well have been that their profession made them
expect that any attempt by the King's mistress to get
back into the country would involve a disguise and false
papers. In actual fact, Helena came quite openly, travelling on her own passport. Using the ordinary train from
Italy, she reached Bucharest unobserved.

On Maniu's return from holiday he was told that

Madame Lupescu had been living at the Foishor Palace since August 4th.

He also learnt that the King no longer desired to hear anything about the Coronation, nor did he want even the farce of a formal reconciliation with Helen to be discussed.

10

CAROL was thirty-seven years of age when he became King. There was a certain regal splendour about his personal appearance—the heritage of his English mother, his German father, and his Russian grandmother. His light blue eyes showed great intelligence. His fair hair was always meticulously groomed and he was extemely proud of his small moustache. But the delicacy of his features were, however, already beginning to disappear under a certain amount of flesh.

He was deeply conscious of the part he had to portray as a King and he preferred to appear in public in uniform whenever he was able, usually in that of the Rumanian Air Force.

He made no attempt, even from the outset, to show a conciliatory attitude to others or to be amenable to any suggestions. He had, at any rate during the first few months of his reign, little time for the flattery of minor politicians who hoped to gain ascendancy under the new monarch.

Carol was fully aware of the truth of the proverb that "A change of rulers is the joy of fools", and he dealt curtly with those who pretended that they were inordinately happy that he had ascended the throne. The result was that he soon became an extremely lonely man, and indeed his only real companion was Helena Lupescu.

The King commandeered for his mistress a small and unpretentious two-storied villa which lay just beyond the grounds of the Palace. Helena furnished it with simplicity and charm. She loved flowers and before the cold of autumn came, she had contrived to fill both the tiny garden and her rooms with masses of pink azaleas.

A lesser woman than Helena might well have vaunted herself in the role of a King's mistress. She secretly gloried in her power as much as any woman would have done in her position, but she was most careful to be discreet.

Although her name and various versions of her life story were known to every man, woman and child in Rumania, there were not above a few hundred people (and even ten years later this number had not increased very greatly) who would ever have recognised her if they had met her face to face.

She appeared at no official function and never openly accompanied her Royal lover on his journeys through his kingdom. But within a matter of days after her arrival in Bucharest, the position inside the Palace was very different.

The handful of Ministers and Court officials who could have personal audience with the King knew her all too well. She was usually somewhere near Carol's study, and the King's visitors quickly learned that it was wise to salute her with deference and to kiss her beautiful white hand before they moved towards the door of the King's study.

Helena Lupescu was the only person Carol would allow to have any influence over him or over his method of government, without feeling suspicion or jealousy. It was for these reasons that soon after he ascended the throne he began to curb his mother's influence.

As a child, Carol had regarded Queen Marie as a goddess. When he discovered at an impressionable period of his adolescence that she was merely a human being who was capable of an illicit love affair, his hatred for her was born. Now that psychological distaste for his mother was somnolent, the hatred was replaced by an equally strong emotion—that of envy.

He recognised that she alone had ever really aroused the devotion of the Rumanian people towards the Royal

House, and he also knew that her influence extended far beyond the borders of Rumania.

The first significant moves of Carol's ill-tempered intolerance were directed towards his mother. He got rid of the Marshal of her Household and other officials, not because they were particularly hostile to him, but because they appeared to be so devoted to her. He ordered police spies to follow many intimate friends of the Queen, and any of importance received an order from him to cease seeing her.

If these crude and unfair activities had been promoted by anyone else other than her son, Queen Marie would have resisted them. However, so anxious was she that Carol should have every chance of making good, that she acquiesced in all that he did and retired gracefully from Society, living in distant parts of the country, and refraining from issuing or accepting invitations.

There remained for Carol the problem of his wife Helen. She proved unexpectedly obstinate. She refused either to state jointly with him that she did not wish for the divorce to be annulled or to co-operate in the provision of evidence to make him the innocent party. The result was that she became a virtual prisoner.

Police patrolled day and night around Helen's house in the Chaussée Kyselef. Her servants were ordered to see that every visitor to the house signed the visitors' book, and the page for each day was taken to Carol. Those whom Carol considered of any importance received orders not to visit the Princess again. She was forbidden to take part in any public ceremony and some of her honorary appointments were cancelled.

The misery of this life wore down her resistance, as it was intended that it should. Helen put in a formal request that she should be permitted to live somewhere outside Bucharest, where possibly she could be granted more freedom of action. The request was rejected and she was told that she had the choice either of continuing to live under surveillance in Bucharest, or of leaving the country altogether. In the second eventuality it was decreed that she must abandon Michael.

The unfortunate woman tried in vain to find a single friend. Even Maniu, who had resigned the Premiership in disgust when he learned that Helena Lupescu was to remain permanently by the King's side, refused to help her.

"The King and you can never live in the same country," he said. "Those were his Majesty's sentiments which he expressed to me. Your Royal Highness must face the fact that it is the King's conviction that your presence prevents him from concentrating on the responsibilities of Government, and that you keep inappropriate devotions alive, so that you are already becoming the centre of opposition to him."

The old man went on to admit that there were many things happening in the country that he had never expected to occur. He believed, however, that it was the duty of every subject of Carol to support him and that anyone who did not obey his wishes was an enemy of Rumania.

In fairness to Carol it must be said that he had under-taken a difficult task at a particularly critical time. When he came to the throne, his country was not only suffering badly from the world economic crisis, but politically it was both torn and weakened by the party conflicts which were aggravated by personal ambition and universal corruption. Carol's eyes turned more and more to events in other more powerful European countries in the hope of discovering something worth imitating.

In Italy, Mussolini seemed to be producing order from chaos. In Germany the first signs of Hitler's growing power were showing with the defeat of the Communists throughout the country.

Carol was a man who, though born to be King, pre-ferred to rule, not by Divine Right, but by popular acclaim and on the strength of his wisdom. He placed his faith in reform. He provided more land for the peasants, breaking up some of the great estates, he ensured that some semblance of free education was available throughout the country for the first time in its history, and above all he developed Rumanian industry.

The result—and it was possibly hardly his fault—was that the reins of Government were transferred from the corrupt, land-owning classes, as represented by the Bratianu dynasty, to the equally corrupt industrialists. At almost frightening speed, Carol began to change from a King ruling through Parliament to a Royal dictator.

He liked to pretend that he was of the people and for the people. He used to boast that he considered himself the First Peasant. Those who opposed him were stripped of power and if they appeared still ready to fight back, they found themselves in prison.

Typical of his ruthlessness was his victimisation of Prince Cantacuzino. A member of one of the oldest and greatest families of Rumanian nobility, he lost most of his income when his estate had been broken up under land reforms. He fell foul of Madame Lupescu. Admittedly there were grounds for believing that he was plotting against her life—this at any rate was the charge on which he was hauled to Court.

Before the agitated judge could prevent him, the Prince claimed that Helena Lupescu had been his mistress, and that when she betrayed him for another, he took the only course open to a man of honour, and that was to try to kill her.

Members of the public in the Court, as well as the jury, were delighted with this ingenious defence. A few believed it to be true and regarded it as a perfectly normal action of a betrayed man. But most of them were too intelligent to think for a moment that there was any truth in his accusation of Helena's infidelity. Even so they admired the adroit manner in which the Prince had turned the tables on the King. The jury returned a verdict of "not guilty" and the judge could do nothing but acquit him.

The Prince died in a mysterious accident shortly afterwards, and Carol made his aged mother, Princess Alexandrine, a prisoner in her own house. Despite protests written formally by Queen Marie, who was a close friend of the old lady, the windows of her home were boarded up, the water was cut off, and no lawyer was allowed to enter.

The opposition to Carol became steadily more formidable. For some years a religious mystical organisation had been flourishing. It was a secret society named the Legion of the Archangel Michael and was basically anti-semitic. The number thirteen was regarded by its members to have a magical significance. Each 'cuib' or nest had thirteen members. A five-fold slogan was chanted at every meeting—"work, silence, education, love, honour."

The moving spirit behind this organisation was a man named Corneliu Codreanu. He had been trained in the legal profession in Germany, but had spent most of his life roaming the mountains of Rumania among the shepherds, or in gaol for every sort of crime, from petty theft to treason. It was said that the finance for his movement came at first from Mussolini.

Codreanu's brand of jingoistic patriotism in his speeches, which were anti-everything and had very little which was constructive about them, appealed to the younger generation. By the time Carol returned to Rumania in 1930, the Legion movement was known as the Iron Guard, and it was said to have had close upon half a million members—an enormous figure in a country with a population of only seventeen millions.

In the spring of 1931, conditions had become so intolerable that Carol decided to dissolve Parliament. He called on Professor Nicolas Iorga to form a Government. Iorga was a literary man and loved by both the upper and lower classes as a true Rumanian patriot. He was the nation's leading authority on Rumanian history and a wise and level-headed man.

At the elections, five Communists got into Parliament for the first time. The Peasant Party suffered a severe defeat and there were a number of successful nominees of the Iron Guard. Carol recognised the new form of opposition that was arising—not that of a handful of powerful individuals, but of large groups of ordinary people. He announced without the permission of Iorga or any Minister that he would personally preside over weekly Cabinet meetings.

By far exceeding any constitutional privilege he had Carol forced through laws designed partly to relieve the economic crisis, which was almost daily getting worse, but also to curry popular favour. He followed the usual dictator's system of defrauding foreign investors and making it wellnigh impossible for international trade to flourish, except on a one-sided system of benefit to Rumanian industrialists.

He dismissed many hundreds of civil servants and replaced them with military officers who had to take an oath of personal allegiance to him. These men were quite incapable of carrying out their jobs, and things went from bad to worse.

For one thing their army pay was far higher than the salary which had been paid to their civilian predecessors, and when Iorga attempted to impose a general cut on Government salaries, Carol vetoed the order, and as a result in June, 1932, the Government resigned.

The National Peasant Party was recalled with Maniu at the head. There were more ominous gains by notorious members of the Iron Guard and by others who blatantly called themselves Fascists in the new Parliament, although the National Peasant Party had a workable majority. With the popular Maniu once again Prime Minister,

Carol considered that this was the opportunity for suppressing the Iron Guard. Soon the prisons were full, but even so the situation was getting completely out of control. The new Government lasted only a matter of six months, and in January, 1933, Maniu once again resigned.

During the elections that followed, more than 18,000 men and women regarded as hostile to the throne were arrested. The new man to pilot the unhappy ship of Rumania through the stormy seas of pre-war European politics, was Ion Duca. He was prepared to be as ruthless as his master, and he announced that like the King's his mortal enemy was the Iron Guard.

Soon after he became Premier, he outlined, with the full approval of King Carol, drastic measures to suppress the movement. He stated publicly, and did not care about the consequences, that the organisation was financed directly by the Nazi Party in Berlin. His activities, brave as they were, were the cause of fatal trouble, both for himself, and in the long run, for his King.

At Christmas, Carol went with Helena Lupescu to spend the holiday at Sinaia. Carol invited his Prime Minister to be his guest for the New Year festivities. Duca went by train and as he left the station at Sinaia to enter the royal car which awaited him, he was shot down by a fusillade of automatic fire.

The three men responsible, high officers in the Iron Guard, continued to pour bullets into the dead body, at the same time holding back railway officials and King Carol's chauffeur, who tried bravely to save the Prime Minister.

The assassins were caught and arrested soon afterwards and a general order went out to capture all members of the hierarchy of the movement. Altogether forty men were listed as due for arrest, and without any doubt, eventual execution.

Codreanu went into hiding until the King and his mistress returned to Bucharest. Evading the cordon which surrounded the city, he then made his way to Helena Lupescu's villa. By bribing the guards he was able to enter her house without warning. A frightened servant told him that his mistress was in bed, but Codreanu pushed him aside and ran up the stairs. He burst into Helena's bedroom.

"I am Codreanu," he said simply. "I warn you that unless you arrange for me to be hidden and protected, you will be assassinated by my legionnaires."

Helena was a woman of great personal courage and it was unlikely that she was intimidated by this threat. She did, however, realise that the Iron Guard movement was now so numerous and powerful that there was no possibility of suppressing it by force. She followed the policy of "kissing the hand that you cannot bite" and was as friendly as possible to Codreanu.

She told him that she believed King Carol and he had much in common, and that if only they could meet, there would be some identity of viewpoint of benefit to themselves and to the Rumania which they both loved.

"Meantime," she went on, "I can arrange for you to be hidden in my father's house. All I ask is that you stay there until I let you know that the King is agreeable to discuss matters with you, when you can surrender voluntarily. I give you my word that your life will not be in jeopardy when you do so."

Few people outside the inner circle of Carol's and Helena's personal intimates knew that her father was living in Bucharest. In fact he had been there for many years and was growing extremely rich by means of the commercial opportunities which came his way through his daughter.

Codreanu was so amazed at Helena's attitude to him, by her fearlessness and by her ready appraisal of his character, that he agreed to accede to her request to go into hiding.

After a few weeks, Helena brought the King to

Codreanu's hideaway in her father's home where she left the two men alone. They discussed politics far into the night, but despite the fact that the King offered what was virtually a partnership in running Rumania, Codreanu was unable to accede to his request to put the Iron Guard under the personal control of Carol. Nothing came of the discussion beyond the promise that at the trial he would be guaranteed an acquittal.

Carol was as good as his word. The next day, Codreanu walked openly into the streets and was promptly arrested. The secret hearing was hurried and no evidence was offered. He was acquitted and once again took over the reins of the Iron Guard movement.

All this time, Carol's battle with his ex-wife continued with unabated vigour. His steady campaign of isolation had at last broken down her resistance and she had agreed to leave the country, abandoning her son to the Court officials. It was agreed that Prince Michael should visit his mother for a period of one month twice a year.

In the autumn of 1932, Princess Helen moved from her exile home in Florence to a quiet hotel in St. James's, London. There she awaited the visit of Prince Michael. The two aides-de-camp who accompanied the boy brought messages from the King that if she allowed him or herself to be interviewed or photographed, the Prince would be immediately recalled to Bucharest.

The arrival of an eleven-year-old Prince, the son of such a notorious father and such a tragic mother, naturally interested the British press and it proved impossible to prevent many photographs being taken. Publication of these in the newspapers of the world brought dire warnings from King Carol that any repetition of this or of similar trouble would result immediately in Prince Michael being forbidden ever to see his mother again.

Immediately after this reproof the unhappy Princess found herself willy-nilly annoying Carol when an invitation came from Buckingham Palace for her to take the

Prince to tea with the King and Queen. The arrangements
for Prince Michael's life in London were so meticulous
that they even included what sort of clothes he should
wear. For some reason better known to Carol, these
included that he should always wear short trousers.

Princess Helen considered that to take a boy of eleven
to tea at Buckingham Palace in clothes which were little
more than a sports dress would be an unwarrantable dis-
courtesy. When the boy appeared all ready for the short
car journey to the Palace, he was in long trousers. The
senior aide-de-camp immediately stated that he could not
go out unless there was express permission from Bucharest.

A telephone call was put through and fortunately there
was no delay in the connection. The aide-de-camp spoke
personally to King Carol, who announced brusquely that
his orders must be obeyed. Prince Michael could go to
the Palace but it must be in short trousers. The Queen
refused to allow the boy to change from the dark suit that
he was wearing and moved from her suite on to the
landing of the hotel, challenging the aide-de-camp
physically to resist her if he wished.

It was, of course, impossible for him to do so and
mother and boy duly set off to Buckingham Palace.
When they returned, the aide-de-camp coldly informed
Helen that Prince Michael was to be escorted home the
next morning. The visit, which by solemn agreement
was to have lasted a month, thus ended in three days.

It was understandable that Princess Helen lost her
temper to such an extent that she immediately arranged
to give a press interview revealing what had happened.
The news made big headlines and was published all over
the world. Her aim, as she stated in the interview, was to
recruit public opinion to preserve the rights which any
mother would claim.

Public opinion may well have been on her side, but the
Government of Rumania was not. Within twenty-four
hours of the article appearing she was given a message

which stated that new restrictions were being added to the agreement as regards the custody of Prince Michael, and also that she would never be allowed to return to Rumania.

Helen determined to call the King's bluff and immediately set out for Bucharest. After a day or two in Paris, she again resumed her journey and arrived at the Rumanian frontier. She was fully prepared for the police to turn her back, but rather to her surprise she was passed through the customs control with every courtesy and deference.

The train, however, was directed from the terminus at Bucharest to a station in the suburbs so that any chance of a demonstration in Princess Helen's favour could be avoided. There, troops in ceremonial dress awaited to escort her to her house in the Chaussée Kyselef. Princess Helen saw, however, that in addition to the escort, in front of the small procession and at the rear, were lorry loads of armed troops in ordinary uniform. She was, in fact, under open arrest.

She soon requested that she might see Prince Michael. whose birthday was rapidly approaching. In order to avoid any public gossip, he was taken most days to see her, but the meeting was always kept to less than half an hour. Then under the pretext that he needed a holiday— a ridiculous excuse because he had only just returned from summer-time vacation near the Black Sea—Michael was sent to Sinaia, where, of course, Princess Helen was not permitted to go.

There was some comfort for the worried mother in the news that at the Foishor Palace at Sinaia her son would be under the care of Queen Marie, who now very rarely appeared in the capital. This, however, did not satisfy her when she learned that Michael had suffered from a serious bout of influenza. Despite strict orders that on no account was she to leave Bucharest, she made her way to the Foishor. She told the numerous officials, who warned her that she was breaking the personal regulations of the

King, that they could if they wished restrain her forcibly.

This, of course, none of them was willing to do, and even though there were minor insults such as the refusal of the taxi driver to take his car through the gates of the Palace, with the result that Princess Helen had to walk nearly a mile to the house, she did see Michael and reassured herself that he was recovering.

Carol was furiously angry when he learned what Helen had done. On her return to Bucharest the guards outside her house were increased and it was made virtually impossible for anyone to visit her.

Wives and daughters of quite unimportant people who wished to see her simply because they were quite unaware of any political implications in their friendship, were soon shown the inadvisability of their actions. Their husbands were dismissed from office or transferred to posts in distant parts of the country.

Carol was prepared to take the most ruthless action to drive the Princess out of the country. He inspired stories in the press that she had attempted suicide, sometimes by an overdose of drugs, sometimes by getting hold of a revolver.

A friendly diplomat told the Princess that it was generally believed in Bucharest that Carol's moves were two-fold, first that the press stories would influence Rumanian people to believe that the King's ex-wife was mentally unbalanced, and secondly that it might place in her mind an idea, which, if she carried it out, would save a lot of trouble all round.

Helen held out for almost a month but eventually she was faced with a Royal edict which in effect said that if she did not go voluntarily, she would be dumped across the frontier. Wishing at least to depart from her son and her adopted country with some dignity, she let it be known that she was ready to go.

Late one night she was taken under police escort to the main station in Bucharest to catch the Orient Express.

Although it was raining and blowing half a gale so that the streets were completely deserted by the public, a line of armed police stood across the entrance to the station, and all the lights inside had been extinguished.

She was escorted to her carriage by the Chief of Police who carried a torch. All railway employees and passengers had been withdrawn from the platform, and she was put in a coach with drawn blinds.

It was really an empty victory that Carol had achieved over his ex-wife. There was no doubt that in the early days there had been little sympathy for her, and most ordinary people had blamed her for the trouble between Carol and herself. Now, however, as details of his callous treatment leaked out, there were more and more evidence indicating that public sympathy was entirely on the side of Princess Helen.

People who had little love for Princess Helen but still less for King Carol, used her as a rallying point for resistance. Dark clouds began to hide the golden tinge which had surrounded the start of Carol's reign. The man who had once known what it was to see peasants kneeling in the dust as he passed by, now found it advisable to move through the streets of Bucharest with a screen of soldiers around him.

By 1934, Carol was busily perfecting his role as a dictator and rapidly turning Rumania into a police state. The postal and telephone services were put under military control and, while for many months international calls had been tapped, now eavesdropping began on local calls.

All freedom of the press was destroyed. Carol issued the most detailed orders on what newspapers could and could not say. Among the hundreds of vetoed names were those of Princess Helen and Queen Marie. His sense of judgment, hitherto so reliable, became completely warped as he experienced the drunkenness of power.

As well as calling himself the First Peasant, he now regarded his role as that of Father to his people—and to him, Fatherhood subconsciously meant the austere and unbending discipline that he himself had known from King Ferdinand.

His conversation with Codreanu had nettled him because he realised that the man exerted an authority which he himself could only attain with the help of police and troops. To compete with the influence of the Iron Guard he organized a youth movement known as the Straja Tarii. He told its officers: "In my country, political parties are sterile and leaders fit only to criticise. It is my business as a King to discipline the people and harness them to constructive work."

The more ruthless Carol's measures became, the more open was the resistance. It penetrated into the Palace itself. An underground movement, partly Communist and partly Nationalist, tried all sorts of subterfuges to annoy the King.

Nothing much could be done in the way of organised revolt, but it was easy to arrange personal pin-pricks against the regime. Most of these were centred around sympathy for Princess Helen.

On one occasion during an outside relay of a speech by Carol in which he arranged pauses so that synthetic applause, based on the Hitler model of broadcast rallies, could be inserted, there came the words "Remember Helen". The slogan was also painted on walls that could be seen from the Palace windows. One night when Carol was having dinner with Helena Lupescu, a tiny piece of paper fell out of his napkin. He unfolded it: and read— "Remember Helen".

There were, however, many who retained their genuine love for both the monarchy and the man who now represented it, and it was with understandable reason that they blamed the change which had come over their King on his mistress.

Partly through his infatuation, and also on account of Helena's increasing greed, she was costing the country an enormous sum of money. It was said that the King gave her the equivalent of £12,000 a year for her dresses, while her jewellery was insured for £50,000.

She was easily the best-dressed woman in Rumania, if not in Europe, at that time. With an inborn good taste and a flair for making the best of herself, she invariably dressed in black. Most of the dresses were made by Chanel. She telephoned her dressmakers, her milliners and her corsetières in Paris every day.

Her figure, now that she was in the thirties, remained slim and beautiful. It had been noticed that before her divorce the weakest feature about her were her legs. According to well-founded rumour in Bucharest, the remarkable slimness of calf and ankle which she had achieved since Carol had ascended the throne, was due to an operation performed by Voronoff, the famous authority on glandular rejuvenation, who was distantly related to her. Whether this was true or not, the fact remained that her once rather fat legs were now beautiful.

Power had undoubtedly tended to change her personality. The once uncannily discreet and deeply affectionate woman, who had said with genuine feeling that she was ready to fade away from her lover's life if it would assist him to regain the throne, was now the real power behind it.

Typical of the influence Helena could exert was an incident which occurred in the winter of 1934. While she still never appeared at official banquets or public ceremonies, she was seen more and more at the numerous private dinner parties which Carol gave at the Palace. She always arrived late at these functions, partly in order to make an entrance and also because she was still acutely sensitive to any possible insult.

By this time, Carol had ordered to be constructed, at a tremendous cost, a tunnel which led from Helena's house under the Palace grounds and into the wing where his private suite was situated. This gave her entrance through a small door in the foyer of the suite, which, on this particular occasion, was being used as a cocktail bar.

Two of the guests that evening were General Antonescu and his wife. The lady was a member of the old Rumanian aristocracy and of a family notorious for its anti-Semitic views. Upon seeing Helena Lupescu, she complained loudly to her husband at the insult of being invited to sit at the table with a Jewess. She called for her cloak and her husband could do nothing but escort her away.

The next day, Antonescu, at the time Chief of the General Staff of the Rumanian Army, found himself demoted and posted to a frontier station. He was replaced by Samsonovici, a man with whom Helena had been friendly in the old days at Jassy.

Samsonovici was not the only man who gained power because of Helena Lupescu's friendship. A far more ruthless and sinister figure was slowly gaining the ascendancy over both the political and military leaders of the Kingdom.

He was an industrialist, a financier and a director of a large number of the companies whose interests covered virtually the whole of the commercial life of the country. Helena had got to know him because he lived next door to her. His name was Ernst Urdareanu.

At that time thirty-five years of age, Urdareanu was a small and swarthy man, dressed in appalling taste. His rouged and powdered face indicated something of his mental and emotional outlook. His rise to power was meteoric and no one, not even Helena Lupescu and the King, had so many enemies. Rumanians nicknamed him "Murdareanu" meaning "dirt". He had a vast amount of cunning, but no mental asset which could really be called intelligence.

Carol did not like Urdareanu but appeared to acquiesce in Helena's wish that he should appoint him as a personal secretary and aide-de-camp. He took over Helena's job of way-laying every person who was given audience with

Carol. There were no letters and no visitors whom he did not see before the King.

While Helena had insisted on politeness and deference before she would influence the King on behalf of a visitor, Urdareanu had more practical ideas. He had to be bribed with money and directorships.

It was said with justification that the shining gold of the Rumanian crown was so tarnished and dull that it could hardly be seen; that the beautiful white hands of Madame Lupescu held the power of life and death; while in the grubby, grasping fingers of Urdareanu lay the fate of the nation. Quite slowly, but inevitably, Carol was sliding to disaster and taking his kingdom with him.

11

1935—1938

A NEUROSIS began to pervade the Court and Government circles, and in its turn this produced instability throughout the country. No one could hope for any security in his post, whether he did well or not. Everything depended on the whim of a woman, the approval of a parasite, and the current temper of the King.

Few people got many thanks for what they did, whether their aim was the disinterested one of patriotism or the more venal one of feathering their own nest.

Ionescu, who had spent so much of his huge fortune in getting Carol back on the throne, was rewarded with the Order of the Thorn, the most distinguished honour that could be conferred in Rumania. For a time he also did well as a box manufacturer with valuable government contracts. But in a very short while, when Carol had no further use for him, the secret police descended on his house and confiscated all gifts and letters which had been given him by the King and Madame Lupescu during Carol's exile.

The only people who benefitted at all were the ruthless and unprincipled men who had, in some way or other, first gained the favour of Helena.

In addition to the powerful Urdareanu, her intimates included Marinescu, the Bucharest Chief of Police. Before Helena Lupescu noticed Marinescu he was an insignificant and impecunious police officer. Within a short time he was one of the wealthiest men in the country.

He took bribes from business men and members of the

army. He was amenable to discussion by political mal-
contents he was supposed to arrest. There was not a
prostitute nor a café proprietor in Bucharest who did not
pay him protection money. It was believed that he
received considerable sums as a spy both for Nazi
Germany and for Soviet Russia.

There was another repellent character in Helena's
intimate circle, a man named Malaxa. He had his finger
in a large number of business activities throughout
Rumania, but his main use to the King's mistress was in
sending money she handed him overseas to be banked in
Switzerland and in a number of states in South America
against the inevitable rainy day.

Many people, with some justification, believed that
Helena Lupescu was uncrowned monarch of the country,
and that she no longer troubled to see that her wishes
were carried out through the King, but was acting direct.

It was perfectly true that without obtaining the King's
permission she had a switchboard put in her house, on
which there were direct lines, not only to the Royal study,
but also to all the Ministries in Bucharest.

When Carol discovered this he made no protest. Nor
did he object openly to the interminable calls that she
made, ringing him up almost hourly throughout the day
to check what he was doing and to advise him on what he
should do. Yet if ever there was a phase in his life when
her hold on him rankled, it was at this period.

The desire to get away from her for a time was one
motive why he insisted on personally attending the funeral
of King George V in January, 1936. He knew only too
well that the King of England had heartily disliked him;
and apart from this, there would have been no breach of
etiquette if he had sent his brother Prince Nicolas, or
even his son. Prince Michael, who was by this time nearly
sixteen years of age and perfectly accustomed to Royal
ceremonial.

Carol's visit to England did him no good, either internationally or among his own people. From the outset circumstances seemed to be against him.

First of all—and with some justification—he considered that the accommodation which had been provided for him in a London private residence was a deliberate slight. He believed that as a reigning monarch of a friendly country he should have been accommodated in Buckingham Palace.

It was one of the many unfortunate occurrences and deviations from the normal which marked from the outset the brief and tragic reign of Edward VIII. Carol could not, of course, know that the slight, if it really existed, was only part of a generally unfortunate pattern.

The next misfortune were the stories that on the two evenings before the funeral, Carol roamed about the West End of London indulging in a drinking bout and eyeing with delight the hostesses in at least two notorious night-clubs. There was no definite proof that he ever visited such places and there was even less proof to substantiate the stories of his behaviour on the day of the funeral.

He walked third in the procession after the nearest male relatives of the dead King—and after the President of the French Republic and the King of Denmark.

As is well-known, there was considerable confusion in the organisation of the funeral procession, and at one point the gun-carriage with the body of King George became separated from the remainder of the procession. King Carol was by no means the only one of the mourners who hesitated, stopped, and sometimes hurried quickly forward on that day.

But only as regards Carol was the disgraceful insinuation made that he was suffering from a "hangover". The story was actually published in the United States, and photographs were printed purporting to show King Carol's personal masseur, who, it was said, having been trying to get his Royal master sobered up right up to the very moment of the procession starting, found himself among a group of foreign dignitaries and was compelled to walk along with them.

There was not an atom of truth in this libellous statement, but of course there was no means for Carol to make any official denial. When he got back to Rumania he found the whole country horrified at his behaviour. It was said that even Helena, by then only too well aware of his drinking proclivities, taxed him with the story and a violent quarrel ensued.

As the months went by, Rumania was of course by no means the only country in Europe which began to slide down the slippery slope to complete chaos. Carol's major mistake had been not to come to some sort of arrangement with Codreanu. It may well have been, of course, that Codreanu's personal ambitions had made such a thing impossible.

He was by this time openly and avowedly an ally of Fascist Italy, then exulting in its victory over Abyssinia, and of Nazi Germany, already preparing to engulf Czechoslovakia. He had changed the name of his organization from the Iron Guard to the "All for the Fatherland" Party.

Aided by lavish sums of German money—on one occasion he received forty million lei (about £40,000) from the German Legation in Bucharest—he had been able to enrol two million members.

In speeches to his recruits he stated openly that within forty-eight hours of coming to power he would announce that Rumania was a Fascist State ready to enter into military alliances with Italy and Germany.

After yet another economic crisis and another fall of Government, Codreanu's party gained sixty-six seats in the elections in 1937, and was thus the second strongest political group in the country.

Helena Lupescu rushed to the King as soon as the election results were announced and warned him that if he did not do something instantly he would find himself either thrown out of the country, or at the very best a puppet like the King of Italy.

Carol heeded her warning but his policy was a disastrous one to the country, even if for a time it saved his own position. Fearful of giving Codreanu any influence or power in the Government, he personally selected a man named Octavian Goga as Prime Minister.

This individual, a poet and political theorist, was so extreme in his views that many people considered him insane. He was a personal friend of Hitler and had enjoyed many conferences with Dr. Goebbels and Hermann Goering. His hatred of the Jews was such that over and over again in articles and speeches, he had advocated the elimination of at least half a million Jews in Rumania as the first measure for restoring the prosperity of the country.

The National Christian Party, which he had formed, contained criminal elements from all parts of Rumania, and for some months had been one of the organisations most closely watched by Carol's secret police.

The whole of democratic Europe was aghast at Carol's move in appointing this man as the principal minister of Rumania. His methods were discussed widely. In the West it was felt that the King of Rumania had become an extreme Fascist.

In Nazi Germany there were considerable misgivings, for the stooge of Berlin had already been carefully selected and trained in the person of Codreanu. Hitler had no desire to see a semi-lunatic as his disciple. But both democracies and dictatorships were agreed on one thing: in Goga, King Carol had a fawning servant who was at least ready to do anything to support the throne. They were wrong.

Carol's behaviour at this time of crisis was that of a cornered tiger—vicious, angry but determined to win. In vain did he explain to Helena—on whom the hopes of the Liberal elements as well as the Jewish section of the

Rumanian community now centred—that his move was to outwit Codreanu and that he was really following the old and well-tried political policy of stealing an opponent's thunder.

"We shall see," said Helena shortly—and for the first and only time in their life together she avoided him.

Her action served both to infuriate and intimidate Carol. There is little doubt that his implicit faith in his destiny as ruler of Rumania had impelled him to take the fantastic risk of unleashing the Fascist forces in the country with the safeguard that he himself could order their master to do his bidding.

He was soon to learn that Goga neither wished to control his henchmen nor to obey his Royal master.

The lonely King sat at his large, eighteenth-century desk, making a pretence of running the country. Sharpened coloured pencils, notebooks and reference books gave the impression of the man of action. Photographs of himself, of Helena, and of Michael, each in a heavy silver frame, hinted at his longing to love and be loved.

Aides came in and placed reports on his desk at frequent intervals throughout the day. He read every word of them, smoking ceaselessly English cigarettes in a long, black holder, and made voluminous comments with his coloured pencils in the margins.

He was at his desk for ten or fourteen hours a day, pretending to himself as much as to others that he was the man of the moment. Not even Helena's forebodings convinced him for some time that he was merely the onlooker at a tragedy on which he himself had raised the curtain.

The days of loneliness and frustration passed by interminably. Friends and enemies noted the absence of Helena from the King's suite. When the servants reported that the discreet visits which had always ended by six in the morning so that the Royal mistress could return to her house before the Palace servants were about had stopped, they contrived to introduce charming girls into the Palace in the hope that Carol might start a new infatuation.

He was courteous to these trespassing sirens. But when they could not give a definite answer to his query as to what they wanted, he smilingly advised them to leave before their presence caused embarrassment and mis-understanding.

At forty-four years of age the King seemed to be as impervious to feminine charms as he had been susceptible to them in his youth.

There was no one in whom he could confide, no one he could trust. Always terrified of the loneliness of spirit which had beset him since he was a child, the most crushing blow he received came in January, 1938.

Helena, feeling the separation as acutely as Carol even though she was determined to hold out for the King's own good, without warning left the country. The train took her as far as Basle on the Swiss frontier, and from there she drove in bitter weather to Paris.

The strain of the journey, and the knowledge that Carol had not as she had hoped thrown aside all else so as to follow her, made her half hysterical when she was met by officials of the Rumanian legation in Paris. They hurriedly began making arrangements to provide her with accom-modation appropriate to their estimate of the King's wishes. But she told them it was unnecessary.

"Regard me as a private citizen of Rumania," she said, her eyes clouded with tears and her characteristic calm-ness breaking down. "This is the final break with His Majesty."

Even when this statement was duly reported to Buchar-est and was referred to the King, he still made no effort to contact Helena personally. He merely gave instructions that Madame Lupescu's financial position and safety were to be his personal responsibility through the Rumanian Legation.

Palace officials were amazed at the King's sang-froid in face of this bitter personal unhappiness on top of all his other sufferings. There were many people who considered that the time was ripe to abandon even lip service to the monarchy and to climb as quickly as possible on to the Goga bandwaggon.

How wrong they were in their assessment of the suave and silent King they learned in February, 1938.

Carol had been abnormally patient with the Goga Government. He had made no protest when it celebrated Mussolini's conquest of Abyssinia. He scribbled his red-pencilled initials of approval when Ion Antonescu, the man he had demoted, was again selected as Minister of War.

He did not even veto Goga's anti-Semitic laws which purged Jews from the professions and many industries. But he pinned to the draft of this announcement when it was submitted to him a cutting from the London *Financial Times*. It reported the spectacular fall in Rumanian loans on every foreign Exchange and Bourse.

Then late one evening Carol acted. The doddering megalomaniac, Goga, was summoned to the Palace. Turning his back on the old man, Carol stated that as from midnight, Goga would cease to be Premier and his Government was dissolved.

Goga took some time to appreciate what had happened. Then he went blundering down the corridor shrieking: "Israel has triumphed!"

He was making too much noise to hear Carol's parting words: "I am master of my country. It is my Government. When I am dissatisfied with its conduct of affairs, I require a change."

The next day, through the Rumanian broadcasting network and by means of a press conference, the King told the nation of his plans. The 1923 constitution was abolished. The new Prime Minister was to be the Rumanian Primate, the Patriarch, Miron Christea. The

(*Right*) Final effort. Carol talks to the Lord Mayor of London at a Guildhall Banquet in November, 1938. The King's hopes of financial aid to withstand Nazi pressure were futile.

(*Photo: Keystone*)

(*Below*) Helena Lupescu (right) with Madame Ionescu in London shortly before Carol was urgently requested to leave the country by the British Government.

(*Above*) Helena Lupescu, Carol and Ernst Urdareanu in Bermuda after leaving Portugal in 1941.

(*Left*) Helena Lupescu no longer objects to press photographers. One of the first of many pictures taken when she and Carol arrived in Bermuda after the flight from Europe in December, 1941.

Ministers of State, personally selected by the King, would represent all parties; they had to be Rumanian for at least three generations and with no connections with any Fascist or Communist organisation.

The Iron Guard had from midnight been an illegal movement, and the instant disbanding of the organisation, with surrender of its arms to the military posts which had been set up in every town and major village at dawn, was a Royal edict.

In Paris, Helena Lupescu exulted at the news. She telephoned Bucharest and in a torrent of loving apologies, said how wrong she had been to consider for a moment that the King had lost his grip on the situation.

And Carol made no recriminations. All he said was— "I need you."

Helena was back at his side within thirty-six hours.

In Britain, Carol's action was approved. While his Government of National Union was nothing but a regal dictatorship, the Foreign Office correctly read into the King's action a consummate boldness in defying the forces of Nazi Germany which had almost gained a stranglehold on Rumania.

From Buckingham Palace came a formal invitation to the King of Rumania to make a State visit to London later in the year.

Carol laughed aloud when he received it—partly with pleasure, but also from the memory of his expulsion by the Special Branch of Scotland Yard. His glee was but a superficial and passing reaction. The invitation was too momentous for anything but gratitude.

The gesture on the part of Great Britain was inspired by an awareness of the imminence of European war. It was sent at the time Hitler was preparing to seize Austria. Even as Carol's reply was sent, the Nazi tanks were rumbling through Vienna, and already there were reports that the aerodromes on Germany's eastern frontiers were being stocked with aircraft. Whether their target was to

F

be Czechoslovakia or all the Balkans was known only to the Fuerher.

In that 1938 summer of crisis following crisis, while almost all Europe shuddered with fear and many foreign ambassadors fawned around the Foreign Ministry in Berlin, Carol II of Rumania touched brief greatness.

Courageously, and despite the warnings given by the swollen staff of the German Legation which he could see from his palace windows, he announced that Fascism was treason.

He personally drew up the plan for the army to swoop on every member of the Iron Guard who was known to be in receipt of Nazi bribes. Codreanu, the man who had once been the King's partner, was among the hundreds arrested. Hundreds more fled across the border into Hungary and thence to Germany.

Carol's preoccupation with politics, the strain of battling with the virtually insoluble economic crisis, and making preparations for war, markedly aged him at this period. There was very little of the Riviera playboy of the twenties about him any more, except that he was still drinking as heavily.

His reconciliation with Helena had been real and deeply comforting to both, but the passionate flavour of their romance had almost disappeared. They had, after all, been in love with one another for more than eighteen years, and had lived together—with breaks of only a few weeks—for sixteen. The fiery sexual desire of the first years had matured into an easy-going and delightful companionship on which both utterly depended.

Helena had once greedily grasped every gift that she could extract from Carol. She had been as ruthless as any of the power-seekers from whom she had accepted what were euphemistically called presents. She had found pleasure in ruining good and decent men simply because they did not pay her the respects due to a reigning consort. Now astoundingly she became a wise and self-effacing helpmate.

True, she arranged for many of her old cronies to retain or attain political power—but the motive was "better the enemy she knew than the friend she didn't." It was also true that she was pessimistic about the future, constantly encouraging Carol to increase his insurance against personal disaster by transferring money beyond the shores of Europe.

At the same time she restrained Carol from many inadvisable excesses, as, for example, in her insistence that the execution of Codreanu might start civil war and would assuredly arouse the ire of Berchtesgarden and Rome. As a result, and to everyone's relief, the Iron Guard leader got off with the comparatively light sentence of ten years' imprisonment for treason.

It was Helena who refused point blank to accompany Carol to London on his State visit. She listened to the schoolboyish plans he had worked out in order to get her into England and installed in a service flat reasonably near Buckingham Palace. She knew that his ideas of her carrying a passport in another name, journeying by a devious route through Europe, and similar subterfuges would have been reported by sources inimical to the throne the moment they occurred. She was also sure that the world's press would be on her trail.

"I shall not accompany you," she said firmly. "I can serve you better here."

Carol was in time grateful for that gesture of self-sacrifice and common sense. He was frankly terrified that his visit, so vital for the future of Rumania, should be marred by the all too familiar slanders and libels, with their consequent reaction in Whitehall.

But if Helena was able to guide her lover wisely through the morass of political intrigue and crisis she was powerless to restrain his inadvisable and petty gestures of hate in more personal matters.

Carol's hostility towards his mother had increased, despite the fact that since 1936, Queen Marie's health had been steadily failing. She never got over her son's unkind gesture in forbidding the women's organisations in Rumania to arrange national celebrations for her sixtieth birthday in 1935.

From that time the Queen Mother lived in self-imposed exile in her villa at Balcic, on the Black Sea coast. The house had been converted from an old Turkish fort, and was built on the steep rocks almost overhanging the sea.

There she had six terraces carved out of the rock, each named after one of her children. They were covered in summer with a profusion of English flowers—climbing roses, irises, and dahlias. The top terrace, on which the house stood, was the Carol Terrace. It was the only one that was left untended after her sixtieth birthday.

In the spring of 1938, Queen Marie's doctors informed Carol that his mother's illness could not be treated in Rumania. They advised that she be sent to a famous clinic in Dresden. For days Carol refused to give permission for her to leave the country, and when finally he did so he made no attempt to see her, although he had been warned that she might not return alive.

He was angered still further when he learned that on arrival at Dresden the Queen Mother had accepted flowers from Hitler, although they had been sent automatically by a Chancellery official as a routine courtesy to a distinguished visitor. Her friendship with Frau Goebbels was, however, not so easily explained away.

That it was merely the groping of a lonely and dying woman towards a little human sympathy and companionship was not for a moment accepted by Carol. Always suspicious, he envisaged some dastardly plotting by his mother in alliance with his enemies.

Instinctively Queen Marie knew that the end was near and she made the painful and exhausting journey home. She reached the Pelishor and was carried indoors in a semi-coma. She died the next day, July 18th.

When he heard that she was really dying, Carol had

rushed to the Pelishor during the night. He was full of contrition, hoping against hope that his mother would regain consciousness so that he could say a few words to her.

Her eyes never opened, but in her handbag with which she had set out on her last journey from Dresden there was found a scrap of paper. On it in almost indecipherably faint letters the Queen had written: "Bury my heart at Balcic."

Carol broke down when he read the message. He knew that the request was not just a sentimental whim, but an exhortation to courage and wisdom. Balcic was part of Bulgaria annexed to form Greater Rumania. It would be among the first places to fall to an enemy in any new war. Queen Marie intended that the brave heart which had inspired her adopted country so strongly through forty years of upheaval and crisis should, in death, be a Rumanian bastion.

Her body was buried in the royal burial place at Curtea de Arges. In the church of the exquisite little Black Sea town with its mosques and fountains, her heart lay in a casket until the war, which just as Queen Marie had feared, wrested Balcic from Rumanian sovereignty.

But before that, Carol had ordered the City of Bucharest to purchase Queen Marie's house and grounds in order to make it civic property. He stated the selling price. He put the money in his own pocket.

12

1938–1939

CAROL's State visit to London was of enormous importance to him. He arranged every detail with meticulous care. Prince Michael, recently given the title of Grand Voivod of Alba Julia, accompanied him. At Helena's insistence, and despite a number of grumbling protests by Carol, Urdareanu was also in the imposing entourage. He had taken for himself the office of Lord Great Chamberlain.

Carol's arrival in London on November 15th, 1938, was perhaps a little too spectacular. In the train from Dover he had put on a musical comedy uniform with a plumed silver helmet and a white silk cloak. But the obviously real and genuine pleasure with which he shook hands with King George VI helped to influence the crowds in his favour. So he received a characteristic London welcome as he brought a theatrical brightness to the foggy winter's day.

Most of his conversations were, of course, in private, but it was soon known that he was achieving little success in obtaining a loan or of improving trade relations between the two countries. Carol spent three days in England, and unfortunately there was practically no benefit from them, either to his country or to his personal cause.

On the second day he was alarmed to receive reports that rioting had broken out in Rumania, and that there had been attacks on Jews all over the country. The attempted rising was, of course, the work of the Iron Guard and it was easy to discover that Berlin had inspired it.

Carol was particularly disturbed when report after report stated that the focal point of all the attacks was Helena Lupescu. Crude caricatures of her had been painted on banners, and everywhere the cry was "Kill the Jewess Lupescu".

He was so worried for her safety that he put through a call to Bucharest which lasted for more than half an hour. He tried to persuade Helena to retire to some secret hiding place or even temporarily to get out of the country. But she laughed away his fears and assured him that she was perfectly safe.

The British press on the whole had been extremely favourable to Carol. Realising that Rumania could be an ally of some importance in Eastern Europe, very few papers made any reference whatsoever to his past rôle as the "Playboy King" or to his mistress. But it was unfortunate that the gossip columns carried a story which showed all too clearly the harsh and ungenerous side of his character.

Princess Helen had been staying in London for some weeks before Carol's arrival. The Rumanian Minister in London was ordered to go to see her and inform her that she would have to leave the country before the King arrived. Helen, who had hoped that she might spend an hour or so with her son, begged that she might be permitted to cross the border into Scotland. She was told, however, that this would not be regarded as obedience to the King's orders. She left for Florence shortly before Carol arrived.

There were some press paragraphs relating this incident, and one or two comments which queried why King Carol had been honoured with the Order of the Garter during his stay—an honour which normally went to men only of the highest integrity and above all of chivalry and moral purity.

The weather was bad during the whole of Carol's stay in London, and it was with a sympathetic depression of the mind that he started back for Rumania. On the way he stopped in Paris where for five days he attempted to obtain loans and concessions of the kind which Britain had not seen fit to supply. There again he was equally unsuccessful. It was with heavy heart that he set out once more—this time to confer with his arch-enemy Adolf Hitler.

The German Fuehrer was at that time residing at Berchtesgaden, and it was in that lofty fortress that the King of Rumania met the leader of Germany. He was insulted immediately on his arrival.

Carol, who was tall and had a really kingly presence when he wished to adopt it, was forced to stand at the bottom of the steps which led to the vast front door of the building. Hitler was standing a few steps higher and he extended his hand condescendingly. The Nazi Press Agency photographers had been stationed even lower down so that the photographs they took gave the impression that Hitler was towering over some midget.

When the Fuehrer had led Carol and Michael into the huge glass-walled reception room which looked over the mountain peaks, Hermann Goering came in. The Field Marshal raised his hand in an ostentatious Nazi salute which the King ignored, extending his hand instead for the normal handshake. Tea was then served, during which Hitler subjected Carol to a long harangue on Germany's destiny. The King bore with it all, then took his cigarette case from his pocket.

"You won't mind if I smoke?" he said, knowing full well that very few people dared to smoke in Hitler's presence. He placed the cigarette in a long cigarette holder, and sat back at ease, smiling.

The Fuehrer, thoroughly put out by this gesture, began to walk up and down the room delivering as he did so a lecture. This consisted of thinly-veiled threats, giving Carol the choice of being destroyed by Soviet Russia which, Hitler said, would inevitably march against all those countries of Eastern Europe which were not under the direct protection of Nazi Germany, or of becoming the satellite of the Third Reich.

Gradually Hitler calmed down, and in an attempt to persuade Carol to come over to his side, began to talk with all the powers of conviction of which he was master. Germany badly needed both Rumania's oil and her farm produce.

With his innate cleverness, Hitler had, in the short time that Carol had been in his presence, accurately estimated that the Rumanian King was no mean adversary, and at the end of the interview came the real sting. Hitler told Carol that his campaign against the Iron Guard was both brutal and ill-advised. He referred in particular to the welfare of Codreanu, who, he said, he believed was suffering severely in prison.

"For reasons of humanity and the welfare of your country, I strongly advise that you release him," the Fuehrer finished.

Carol replied that he thought he was capable of running his country to the best advantage. Whereupon Hitler stood up and indicated that the interview was over.

There were none of the polite conventions normal when one head of a State visits another—no banquet, no meeting with other Ministers of Nazi Germany.

Carol took his leave, and with Prince Michael started on the journey home. On this occasion they travelled via Switzerland, where the King had vague hopes of obtaining financial aid from the Swiss banks as he had been able to do once before.

On arrival, however, there were fresh reports from Rumania awaiting him. The unrest was becoming rapidly more serious. Not only was the Iron Guard busily fomenting trouble throughout the provinces and particularly in Transylvania, but there were indications that mutiny was likely to occur in some sections of the army.

Instead of taking a brief rest at Helena's villa at Vitznau

on Lake Lucerne as he had intended, Carol immediately went back to Rumania. At the border he was met by Calinescu, a good and reliable friend whom he had appointed as Minister of the Interior. The story that Calinescu had to tell was even more serious than Carol might have expected from the reports sent to London and Switzerland.

The Rumanian police had for the most part remained loyal, but they were attempting to put down all disorders by the most ruthless measures. Many hundreds of people had been shot, and the prisons were packed to capacity.

Carol listened in silence to the story as the train continued on its way to Bucharest. When he arrived there on the evening of November 28th, he immediately summoned a Crown Council. By midnight its decisions were in operation.

A number of highly-placed officers in the army were routed out of bed and taken to prison. Squads of armed police raided warehouses and private houses, capturing large numbers of documents and supplies of propaganda literature. More members of the Iron Guard were rounded up and as the prisons could no longer hold them, they were placed in confinement in army barracks.

All the next day, Carol never left his desk even for a meal. Helena Lupescu brought him sandwiches and black coffee, and was rarely far from his side. But in late afternoon he insisted that she should leave him alone, as he had some special arrangements to make on which he alone wished to take responsibility, should anything go wrong.

A number of trusted officials of the secret police and two officers of his own regiment were summoned to the Palace with orders to approach by the rear entrance. Carol was in conference with them for just over an hour. They left singly and as secretly as they had come.

Late that night an army lorry rumbled up to the gates of the prison where Codreanu and 13 of the leading members of the Iron Guard, including the murderers of the Prime Minister a year before, were held in custody. The Governor of the prison was presented with an order signed by King Carol to hand over his charges for transfer to the Jilava prison some distance from Bucharest.

Fourteen picked troops were in the lorry and each took charge of one of the prisoners. Behind the first lorry was another one on which another group of troops stood, each armed with an automatic weapon. Behind that was a third vehicle which contained nobody but the driver. Its load was concealed under heavy tarpaulins.

The convoy started out and immediately took to narrow roads and tracks for its slow journey to Jilava, avoiding the direct route in case anyone in the prison had informed Iron Guardists of the chance of rescuing their leader and his principal lieutenants.

For hour after hour the lorries rumbled around until they were some thirty miles from Bucharest. They passed through the village of Tancabesti and then reached a heavily wooded area. Here the lorries were compelled to slow down because of the terrible condition of the road. From the trees came a burst of gunfire.

As pre-arranged, the lorries stopped. The prisoners, despite the fact that they were bound, believed that rescue was imminent and began to shout for help. Immediately each guard, with a leather strap which he had been given when he started out, strangled his prisoner.

The troops in the second lorry jumped out and began running up and down the road firing sporadically in all directions, so as to give the impression to anyone living nearby that there had been some sort of ambush. Then the lorries continued on their way and just as dawn was breaking, reached Jilava jail, with their cargo of corpses.

There the troops dug a mass grave in an exercise field within the prison walls. The bodies were thrown in and acid poured over them. From the third lorry sacks of cement were taken and their contents thrown over the bodies. Then the grave was filled with water. Half an hour later the soil and turf were replaced and the job was over.

Carol had given orders to his propaganda office to see that the Bucharest newspapers delayed publication for two hours that morning. In the editorial offices the staffs awaited the important news that had been promised. Before mid-morning the special editions were on the news stands announcing that Codreanu and thirteen other criminals of the Iron Guard had been shot while attempting to escape.

The country was aghast at the news. Few believed that the reason for the mass killing was that which had been given. There were too many instances of prisoners being mown down when they had allegedly attempted to flee for liberty for anyone really to believe that this was the genuine motive. But the announcement certainly had the desired effect of stopping instantly all the unrest in the country.

Just to show that the destruction of Codreanu was no isolated gesture, a special order of the day was publicly issued to the police. It said:

"From the date of this order the most determined measures are to be taken immediately against persons guilty of violence. Terrorists are to be attacked at once without any need to comply with the normal regulations for a warning before shooting. No mercy should be shown in the steps taken to maintain law and order. No police officer need show the slightest hesitation or weakness in carrying through this order. It must be a point of honour with every officer to suppress every attempt at violence with the utmost ruthlessness."

Within a fortnight, Carol had appointed himself dictator of Rumania. He announced the formation of a new party called "The Party of National Rebirth". There was no permitted opposition and at the elections the new Government was naturally put in with an overwhelming majority. The new Prime Minister was Calinescu.

Whatever esteem the King gained among the Western democracies for his courageous resistance to Nazi aggression, the ruthless measures which he had taken and the formation of a State closely modelled on the Italian pattern did not enhance his personal prestige at a time in history when the whole of the world was moving into two camps.

Whether Carol was an enemy of Hitler or not, he did himself little good by imposing a dictatorship on his country. Nevertheless his heavily reinforced squads of armed police managed to maintain an uneasy peace throughout the kingdom. Few thinking people inside or outside Rumania, however, could believe that he was really winning the battle.

When in March, 1939, Hitler annexed Czechoslovakia, the situation immediately became serious. Large numbers of German divisions were massed within striking distance of the Rumanian border. In Hungary and Bulgaria, troops equipped with German arms and largely officered by German personnel stood ready to regain the territories which their newspapers proclaimed day after day had been stolen by Rumania.

There was nothing for Carol to do except to agree to the trade agreement which was forced on him by Berlin. Oil, wheat, maize and soya beans had to be exchanged for whatever Germany wished to send them—mostly tawdry household gadgets and toys, and truckloads of aspirin. It became a national joke to talk about Carol's headache which even the massive supplies of drugs which Hitler had kindly sent him could not cure.

Some relief of his troubles occurred on April 13th, 1939, when Mr. Neville Chamberlain, as Prime Minister, announced in the House of Commons that Great Britain would guarantee the independence of Rumania against any aggressor. The British Prime Minister also stated that an economic mission would leave for Bucharest immediately.

But the offer of political alliance should war come was, of course, merely a gesture of support. Nothing could really be done for Carol. The economic aid for which the King had hoped was equally nebulous. His envoys were still negotiating supplies of arms and aircraft when war was declared in September, 1939.

During the months which preceded the second World War Carol had worked so hard that he was mentally and physically exhausted. At Helena's urgent suggestion he agreed in July to go for a cruise with her. Against his better judgment he agreed to her pleadings, and together they set out for Constanta where his yacht *Luceafarul* was kept.

This was the famous vessel formerly known as the *Nahlin* which had been used by the Prince of Wales on his holiday in the Aegean Sea with Mrs. Simpson. Carol had purchased it because Helena had been so intrigued by the romance of the Duke of Windsor. She had told Carol that the yacht which had served the British Royal lovers so well would also be an ideal refuge for them.

Although Carol had owned the *Luceafarul* for nearly two years, he had never found the time to go to sea in her. Now he and Helena had a leisurely and pleasant holiday cruising through the Aegean, and then to Crete.

Often in the dark and tragic days which followed he recalled with delight those happy weeks away from the cares of State.

"I think this trip was the happiest time during the whole of my reign," he was accustomed to say.

Three weeks after the holiday was over, Europe was at war. There was nothing for Carol to do and indeed no reason for him to make any useless gesture of defiance. It was announced that Rumania intended to remain neutral. At the same time, Carol put in hand vast defence works in all the vulnerable areas on Rumania's borders.

On the morning of September 21st, 1939, he had an audience with his Prime Minister, Calinescu, at the Cotroceni Palace. Their conversation was satisfying, for the country appeared to be quiet and the defence works were well in hand.

"You see now, my friend," said Carol, "how wise was my policy in getting rid of Codreanu and cutting the claws of the Iron Guard. At least we shall have no more trouble on that score."

Calinescu murmured his agreement and left the Palace. Ten minutes later he was dead.

As his car was passing through the centre of Bucharest, a cart turned right across the street, blocking the way. Calinescu's chauffeur pulled up sharply and immediately a torrent of gunfire poured bullets into the body of the Prime Minister.

Fifteen minutes later more men rushed into the studios of the Bucharest radio station and at pistol-point forced their way into the room where a programme of gramophone records was being given. Grabbing the microphone, one of them shouted into it:

"The death of Calinescu has been achieved. Codreanu and his Iron Legion are revenged."

Carol lost his head. Although he was able to suppress any further trouble, the country was horrified at the ruthlessness of his measures. Anyone suspected of complicity in the crime, or of being an active member of the Iron Guard, was arrested, tried by a military tribunal and shot immediately.

The alleged assassins of the Prime Minister were taken to the street where they had committed their crime and executed there. Their bodies, by Carol's explicit orders, were left lying in the street for twenty-four hours afterwards.

The funeral of Calinescu was made an excuse for a

tremendous display of force. Prince Michael and all the leading members of the Government, the Army and the Church were in the procession. Carol himself did not dare to participate.

He sent an empty carriage to represent him.

13

I T was not unnatural that at this time, Carol became almost unbearable to live with. Helena adopted the rôle of·a devoted servant rather than a mistress. She hovered discreetly in the background, seeing to it that he had his meals, and trying to prevent him over-straining himself.

Paradoxically the stimulant which Carol was coming to rely on more and more to outwit the Nazis was the German pep drug Pervitin which contained enormous quantities of Vitamin B1.

He, in his turn, managed to find time from all the onerous duties of statesmanship to worry about Helena's welfare. He had good reason for this because the campaign of slander and innuendo against "the Jewess Lupescu" had reached tremendous proportions.

In Germany and all the States under her control, a stream of filth was poured out revealing the alleged sins of the King's mistress. Magazines and pamphlets were surreptitiously distributed throughout Rumania in which every suffering endured by everyone in the whole country was ascribed to the machinations of the insidious Royal mistress.

Dr. Goebbels had scoured Himmler's concentration camps to find a Jewish woman with features vaguely like those of Madame Lupescu. The woman he selected served as a model for the photographs which were repro-duced by the million.

As few Rumanians had ever seen Helena Lupescu, and the King had unwisely forbidden the Rumanian press ever to publish the few photographs they had taken of her, the majority of the ordinary people implicitly took the Nazi propaganda pictures as authentic.

Hair-raising stories of her extravagances and the hypnotic power she exerted over the King and his cronies steadily achieved the desired end: Helena Lupescu was the fount of all evil in Rumania.

The King, who was able to withstand the calumnies hurled at his own head, was greatly disturbed by the attacks on his mistress, and once again he endeavoured to persuade her to leave the country. Helena as usual insisted that her place was by his side.

If the truth were told, Carol really had no defined policy by this time, and he was vacillating from one idea to another in a frantic endeavour to retain the independent existence of his country. As the Nazi campaign grew in intensity, he suddenly switched around and virtually went into the German camp.

In March, 1940, he stated that there would be a complete amnesty for prisoners of the Iron Guard. So long as they swore allegiance to the Crown they could be assured of complete legal and political privileges within the country. Thousands of men and women were released and many hundreds reinstated in their former posts in the Government and in the Army. Carol had sold himself body and soul to Nazi Germany.

He believed that in return there might be a gesture of friendliness from Berlin and that the campaign against Helena would cease. For a time, at any rate, events proved him right. The German press soft-pedalled its revelations about the King's private life and the smuggling of anti-Lupescu propaganda into Rumania ceased.

The country was quiet, and there was a semblance of prosperity as war increased the prices for the flood of food and oil which went to Germany. Carol felt particularly happy early in the morning of May 10, 1940, as he prepared himself carefully for a review of his troops outside the Cotroceni Palace.

He wore the same musical comedy uniform which he had displayed to the crowds at Victoria station in the winter of 1938. He was striding up and down in front of an admiring Helena when a servant entered with a report which had just been hurriedly prepared by his Foreign Ministry. It told him that at dawn that morning the Nazi armies had invaded Holland and Belgium and were said to be advancing westwards into France.

Carol tried to convince himself that the end of the 'phoney war' in the West was an advantage to Rumania. While the Nazi war machine was busily occupied against France and Great Britain, Rumania could buy a little more time. He went out of the palace, mounted his white charger, and with Prince Michael by his side, rode to the parade ground. There for several hours he took the salute of the army he had created.

As his passably well equipped and disciplined troops passed by, Carol told himself that there would be very little likelihood of their ever going into action. Neutrality was his policy, and he believed that he could ensure that it continued until the war was over. Of the ultimate victory of the Western democracies, despite the alliance between Rumania's neighbours, Greater Germany and the Soviet Union, he had no doubt.

But within six weeks Carol abruptly changed his mind. Hitler had destroyed Belgium and the Netherlands. Norway was his. The greater part of France was a German colony and Britain was preparing to defend herself against invasion.

In the thoughtless manner that was so much a part of his character Carol switched his policy. He announced on July 21st what amounted to the unconditional surrender of Rumania to Hitler. He proclaimed the creation of yet another new Party, "The Party of the Nation", which was to all intents and purposes, the Iron Guard.

The new power behind the throne was the Minister of Culture, Horia Sima, the leader of the Iron Guard. This man, trained by the Nazi College for so-called Supermen in Germany, was at that time thirty-four years of age. He was intelligent enough not to worry about Helena Lupescu's alleged non-Aryan ancestry but to make her his good friend. It was with her help that he persuaded Carol to repudiate the treaty between Rumania and Great Britain and to expel the British engineers who had run the Ploesti oil fields for more than twenty years.

Horia Sima also drew up new and more stringent anti-Semitic laws excluding Jews from any position in the press, the theatre and commerce. Yet Sima was not the boss of Rumania. His real masters were to be found in the German Legation and in the building of the German Economic Commission in Bucharest.

At the Legation, Sima used to have daily conferences with Conradi, the head of the secret Nazi party of Rumania. This man, unknown even to Carol, was one of the most menacing figures in the tragedy which was being played out in Bucharest. Paralysed from the waist downwards, he had an enormous head on a tiny body. Grotesque and sinister, he would boast that he was without pity, without mercy, and without remorse.

The head of the German Economic Commission which worked in a building immediately opposite the Ministry of Culture in the Strada Wilson was Dr. Neubacher. He had once been mayor of Vienna and was a handsome blond German in his middle forties. Carol liked him and often had him to dinner, largely, it was said, because Dr. Neubacher's wife was an extremely pretty Viennese and had an even more beautiful daughter. When they were guests at the palace, Helena Lupescu always found an excuse to be elsewhere.

While Carol was busily making overtures to Nazi Germany in order to prevent the rape of his country, Moscow was hatching its own plot. Late on the night of June 26th, Molotov issued an ultimatum to the Rumanian Minister, stating that the Soviet Union wished to settle the question of the restoration of Bessarabia to the Soviet Union, as well as the future of Northern Bucovina. The Government of Rumania was given twenty-four hours in which to reply.

Carol remained up all night discussing the situation, but he was inevitably compelled to suggest even partial agreement, asking for a little time so that friendly discussions could proceed in due course. Moscow's answer was to insist on Rumania's instant agreement that the transfer of territory should be completed within four days.

All that Carol could do was to announce his acceptance of the conditions in order to avoid serious consequences for the population.

The entire country was roused in a fury of anger and disappointment that Carol had given way so easily. They could not know that the King had urgently telephoned Hitler, begging for some gesture from the Fuehrer so that at least he could make a show of resisting the Soviet Union's claims.

The telephone call had been difficult to put through because Hitler was at that time in some secret headquarters in France, planning the Battle of Britain. Even when the connection was made the Fuehrer refused to speak to the King. After four hours, while Carol never left his desk, a message came through just before midnight when the Russian ultimatum was expiring.

It stated: "The Fuehrer orders the Rumanian Government to cede Bessarabia and Northern Bucovina without fighting."

There was no question of suggestion or advice. It was an order from the Dictator of Germany to the man he regarded as his lackey, the King of Rumania.

In the disputed territories, the refugees had begun to cross the border the moment the Soviet ultimatum had been published. They were only too well aware of the probable outcome. Many of the wealthier landlords were of German origin, minor princes and counts, who had been privately informed by the German Legation in Bucharest that it would be advisable for them to get out as the Fuehrer was going to insist that Rumania yielded the territories to Russia.

These people, refugees in name, but in fact moving in expensive cars and with convoys of lorries conveying their possessions, made infinitely more fuss than the patient peasants trailing miserably along the roads. Carol had little doubt that Germany would look after them.

The real seriousness of the situation was, as he well knew, that with the loss of these territories, Rumania was deprived of nearly a quarter of her wheat supplies, a third of her sugar beet, the best of her sheep, and most of her soya bean crop. Greater Rumania, born of the first world war, was losing 2,000 square miles of land and three-and-a-half million inhabitants to the Communists.

On the afternoon of June 28th the King called a meeting of the Crown Council. It was an occasion that he was long to remember. The day was hot and sunny. Inside the palace all was serene and peaceful as the white-uniformed servants escorted the Ministers to the lift which bore them to the Great Conference Room on the first floor.

Carol sat at the head of the table and on his right was Urdareanu. The first person to arrive was the Patriarch of the Church, on this momentous occasion, wearing his gold tunic under a black cloak. Maniu, now sixty-seven years of age and weak from a long period of illness, arrived next. It was the first time that they had met for many months, and Carol was greatly moved by the warm and comforting handshake which the old peasant leader gave him. There were tears in their eyes as they discussed the situation.

Tartarescu, at that time the acting Prime Minister, was the third to arrive. He was quickly followed by the other Ministers and Carol's military advisers, all of whom, almost to a man, were ready to be German collaborators.

Carol gave a frank and reasonable outline of what he had been doing and what he had failed to do. For once there was perfect unity around the table, for in this moment of crisis, all the petty jealousies and intrigues for and against Carol were forgotten.

None of the members of the Council was unkind enough to say what was in all their minds—that the King had put himself in the grip of forces which had now got completely out of control. Even those whose sense of patriotism was distorted by an admiration of Hitler's New Order had a certain twinge of remorse at the disaster which was overwhelming their country.

In any event they could make no criticism of Carol on this score. For it had seemed obvious—ignoring for the moment the treaty between Hitler and Stalin—that no one could possibly have done more in the past few weeks to placate the German dictator than Carol.

When at the end of the long and more or less purposeless conference, Ion Gigurtu—one of the most recent of the long succession of Prime Ministers appointed by Carol—announced that in his opinion the only possible future policy for the nation was to put itself entirely in the hands of Germany, there was surprisingly little protest. Even the King, hitherto so jealous of retaining any such major suggestion of policy for himself, merely mumbled an affirmative.

In reality this was the day when Carol abdicated, even if the formal gesture of doing so was still some distance away.

After the members of the Council had left the Palace, Carol went to his own study. Helena was awaiting him there and she was horrified at his bent shoulders and dragging footsteps. He was a beaten man. She took him across to a sofa beside the window and in the cool of the evening breeze, she tried to comfort him, stroking his head and telling him that whatever happened they still had each other.

Her words, from a woman then approaching her middle forties, were almost pathetic in their futility and in their unnaturally youthful optimism that all would come right. But her sympathy had the desired effect on Carol. He became optimistic once more and shortly afterwards managed to eat a good dinner.

It was during the meal that Urdareanu entered and said that General Ion Antonescu was asking for an audience. Helena had never forgotten nor forgiven the insult she had suffered from the General's wife, while Carol had developed an immovable fixation that Antonescu was largely responsible for all the political trouble which thwarted him inside the country.

Urdareanu, who was jealous of anyone who might influence Carol and displace him as the major personality in the King's entourage, advised his Royal master that it would be inadvisable to accede to the request for an audience. To this, Carol gladly assented.

With a grin of triumph Urdareanu left the room and went downstairs to the entrance hall to convey the King's message in as insulting a manner as possible. Antonescu was impatiently pacing up and down. He had never anticipated for a moment that whatever difference of opinion there might have been between the King and himself in the past, at this terrible time his offer of help would be rejected.

When Urdareanu gave him the message, he protested, demanding to know the reason. Urdareanu let it be known that it was he himself who had decided on behalf of the King that there should be no audience. In reply the hot-tempered General smacked Urdareanu across the face with the back of his hand. Immediately Urdareanu smacked Antonescu back, and soon they were fighting like a couple of peasants.

None of the servants of the Palace standing around

dared to separate them. The General pummelled the politician almost into unconsciousness, after which, satisfied with his gesture of defiance, he left.

When the King and Helena were told of the fight, Helena was all for immediate reprisals, but Carol pointedly refused to do anything. The fact was that for a long time he had become tired of Urdareanu, if only because of the almost hypnotic influence he had over him.

On the following morning Carol sent a summons to Antonescu to come and see him. The General arrived in civilian clothes to indicate that he was speaking as an ordinary Rumanian subject and not as an officer.

"Your Majesty," he began in a broken voice, "the country of Rumania is crumbling into ruins. The scenes in the area of your kingdom which have been yielded to the Soviet armies are a heart-breaking tragedy. Civil servants who have loyally tried to carry out your orders have been abandoned and officers alongside whom you once fought, have been stripped of their badges of rank and deprived of their arms.

"Seizing of these rich territories of yours has occurred before the harvest was taken in and a large proportion of the food which would have been needed to feed your armies and your people during the coming winter has been lost. It is perhaps inevitable, but at the same time the Russian authorities have deliberately prevented the trains and convoys of lorries already loaded with goods from your factories from passing into what remains of Rumanian territory.

"It is my duty and privilege to tell you, Sire, that the people beyond the borders of the Russian annexation now completely lack confidence in the members of your Government. Even in this city of Bucharest the hatred against the men who have been guilty of misleading you and of doing this dastardly thing increases minute by minute."

Carol remained completely silent. He made only a weary gesture with his hand without looking at the General, that he should continue.

"I tried to warn your Ministers about this and was, as a result, treated as a rebel," Antonescu went on angrily. He collected himself and came closer to the King, "I am not looking for revenge on that," he added more calmly, "I only want to save what is still left to be saved of your Majesty's crown, of our country, and of our frontiers.

"I have never been an enemy of your Majesty. I have always been a faithful servant of the Rumanian nation. I beg of you, your Majesty, that you listen to me in this terrible moment of our history. Intrigue in the past has ruined my career. Do not allow intrigue to ruin your Majesty's life too. I beg you not to listen any more to those people whose loyalty has been bought by politicians beyond the borders of Rumania. This is my last plea to you."

For fully two minutes Carol said nothing and made no movement. Then, fixing his light blue eyes with their piercing frankness and intelligence on the General he said:

"I admire you for your courage in coming and saying all this to me. I shall not forget your words." Twenty-four hours later, members of the personal body-guard of King Carol went to Antonescu's house and arrested him. He was thrown into the Manastirea prison without trial.

Within a week, Carol had proclaimed the official adherence of Rumania to the Rome-Berlin axis. He announced that Rumania was now a satellite of the Third Reich. He made a silly and unnecessary gesture of bravado by stating that from July 10th Rumania would no longer be a member of the moribund League of Nations.

If he had thought that with these slavish tokens of his esteem for Hitler and Mussolini he was successfully rescuing his kingdom from further disaster, he soon learned how wrong he was.

On orders from Berlin, Hungary began to demand the
return of Transylvania. After the Hungarians had rattled
the sabre for a reasonable period, the Berlin Foreign
Ministry announced that it would assist the two disputing
nations to come to a reasonable arrangement. A conference would be held in Vienna on August 30th.

The Rumanian Premier and Foreign Minister went to
the Belvedere Palace in Vienna and with their opposite
numbers from Hungary sitting on the other side of the
room, awaited patiently the arrival of the German representative. They were kept waiting more than an hour.
When the door opened, it was Ribbentrop himself who
walked in. Behind him came Count Ciano representing
Italy.

Ribbentrop glanced impatiently at his wrist-watch and
as if he had far more important matters to attend to than
a minor problem of this kind, took a small sheet of paper
from his brief-case and began reading it.

"By order of my Fuehrer, Adolf Hitler," he said, "the
German nation offers you two alternatives—either that
you accept the boundary which is indicated on a map
that you can shortly study, or troops of the Third Reich
will march alongside their comrades in arms of the Hungarian regiments into Rumania."

Ribbentrop nodded a formal farewell to the astounded
delegates and left the room.

14

1940

THE news from Vienna on the morning of August 31st, 1940, confirmed to Carol what in his heart he had known for some time—that his reign was ending. But he was a gambler, and with a gambler's optimism he still hoped for some miracle. He tried to tell himself that war could achieve the impossible.

When the Rumanian delegates arrived back from Vienna early in the evening he summoned the Crown Council. He himself advocated a rejection of Hitler's ultimatum, even at this late hour. The Rumanian officers, only too well aware of the condition of the country's defences, warned the King that, if he did this, defeat would be swift and complete.

Before the conference ended, Carol was showing signs of strain. His hair was tousled and he was unshaven. In front of him stood a bottle of whisky, which he had almost emptied.

In slurred speech he talked alternately of his optimism that everything could come all right if only they would act as true Rumanians, and in the next breath hinted that he intended to commit suicide. The Councillors ignored his plea, and indeed the only person wholly on his side was the aged Patriarch who continually begged the King not to sign any document harming either himself or the Kingdom of Rumania.

At the last moment, as Carol looked round the table and saw the resolute and critical faces of the men in whom he had entrusted the Government of his country, he suddenly stood up and ran into his own study. Nonplussed, the Councillors sat on for half an hour wondering what was afoot.

In the other room Carol was telephoning to his
Ambassador in Moscow attempting to get a military
alliance with the Soviet Union. It was, of course, a
melodramatic action about which presumably the
Rumanian envoy did nothing. At any rate the King
returned to the Council Chamber, slumped in his chair,
made a gesture of hopelessness and let it be known that
he was ready to hear the voting.

He looked up only when the Patriarch, tears rolling
down his parchment cheeks, said that the vote was carried
in favour of immediate acceptance.

The delegates shuffled out of the room and left Carol
to his thoughts.

Neither Helena nor Urdareanu dared to approach
him at this time of mental and emotional conflict. The
King walked to the windows which were wide open, for
the evening was hot and oppressive with the heaviness of
thunder in the air. Outside, beyond the trees, as he stood
carefully to the side of the window so that he could not
be seen, he stared at the Royal Square surrounded by
masses of gladioli, at that time in the full glory of their
bloom. To one side stood a huge bronze statue of Carol I.

It had always been the King's secret hope that before
his death the Rumanian people would demand that a
similar statue of himself should be placed on the other side
of the Square.

Carol drank in the scene of his capital with all the
eagerness of a man who wished to record every detail in
his memory before it was too late. He had done much to
change the centre of Bucharest since he had ascended the
throne. Three times he had torn down the frontage of the
Palace and had it reconstructed according to his current
whim.

On this September evening when all his hopes and
ambitions were crashing in ruins, he could see the
scaffolding, the building material and the workmen's
huts left as they had abruptly stopped work, owing to the

need for the construction of defences on the borders of the country.

He moved away from the window and sat down once more in his chair at the head of the empty conference table. He finished the remainder of the whisky at a gulp and then went to his study.

Although only fifteen or twenty minutes had elapsed since the Councillors had left, the radio which he turned on was already interrupting its programme to report the triumphant bulletin which had been broadcast by the German and Hungarian networks a few minutes before. Then above the noise of the radio came the sound of shouting and above that a heavy rumble.

The study windows looked out over the rear of the palace grounds, and to see what was happening, Carol returned once more to the Council Chamber. Masses of people were converging on the Royal Square from all directions, shouting and screaming.

The tone of the mob's noise was low and menacing— a sort of human baying for blood. Carol saw that some of them were carrying banners on which had been painted the crude caricatures of Helena Lupescu and Ernest Urdareanu. Their names being screamed by the crowd were just audible above the cacophony of sound.

Carol grasped avidly at the fact that there was no banner on which his face had been portrayed, and, so far as he could hear, none of the vituperation included his name.

The rumbling got louder. As he watched, the crowds began to scatter in all directions. Along the Calea Victoriei and from a number of side roads, tanks were coming at full speed. Each machine was towing a water carrier and when the tanks reached the Square, powerful jets were sprayed in all directions. It was all over in a matter of five minutes. The tanks remained in the deserted Square for a little while and then they too rumbled away.

No one came to tell Carol of what had happened. A

sickened and weakened man, he passed from the Council
Chamber. Ignoring the flunkeys who stood impassively
along the corridor he made his way to the tunnel which
he had built near the palace kitchens to connect with a
small villa where, for the past two or three years, he had
been living. This was known as the New House and was
also joined to the original tunnel Carol had constructed
to Helena Lupescu's house.

In his villa he found Helena awaiting him. She had
prepared a meal for him with her own hands—a simple
dinner just like that which he had enjoyed those many
years ago at Jassy. He tried to eat some of the food but
stopped when the ever-intruding radio announced that
the Foreign Minister, Manoilescu, had an important
announcement to make.

In slow and solemn words, with his voice often breaking
through emotion, Manoilescu told of the tragedy that
had occurred. He did not minimise the extent of the
disaster, listing the details of the land and people who
were being wrested from the Kingdom of Rumania.

Before the terrible schedule had been completed, Carol
had switched off the radio and sat like a man in a trance,
staring ahead of him, oblivious of the comforting gestures
and whispered sympathy of Helena.

The next two days brought a sort of stunned reaction
when things were comparatively quiet. But slowly the
anger of the people became more pronounced, fanned as
it was by the Iron Guard. Resolutions were passed that the
King must go. In many provincial cities and in the
industrial areas of Bucharest, there was sporadic fighting,
and at night occasional shots could be heard.

The Bucharest radio station went abruptly off the air
when a group of Iron Guardsmen forced their way in.
They were easily repulsed by army sentries, and the
programme was resumed after not more than two minutes'
interruption. But the listening public knew the significance
of that unexplained break.

Still Carol received virtually no information of what was going on, not only because he no longer counted for very much, but on account of the absolute panic of the Gigurtu cabinet. It was frankly terrified of the Iron Guard and wished fervently that the organisation would take over the direction of the country.

On the evening of September 3rd, Carol collected himself and took action. He called in the Chief of Police and told him personally to go and release Antonescu from prison.

Soon afterwards the palace telephones went out of action. The Iron Guard had taken over all the exchanges in the country. Still the position remained comparatively quiet. There was hardly any traffic passing through the Royal Square, and all that could be seen in the twilight as night fell were the figures of armed police and troops patrolling slowly up and down. Rumania was waiting.

On the next day the Gigurtu cabinet resigned and Carol sent trusted emissaries to Antonescu's house asking him to come to see him. It was his last frantic effort to retain his throne and to regain at least a semblance of control over the country. Antonescu had not forgotten what happened after his last audience and he insulted the King by sending a message that he would not find it convenient to attend at the palace until noon on the following day.

Carol managed to control his temper. And that evening he insisted that Urdareanu should resign from the position of Court Chamberlain.

"It will be wise for you to do so," he said wryly. "You are hated second only to me."

Sullenly Urdareanu agreed and stole away to make his own arrangements to save his carcass. Gone was any of his pretended devotion to Rumania.

Carol put on the uniform of a Field Marshal with all the insignia of his rank as Commander-in-Chief. Antonescu arrived in a car which moved slowly so that an

(*Right*) Helena Lupescu in Rio de Janeiro a photograph taken at about the time of her marriage.

(*Left*) Safe—and half-forgotten. Ex-King Carol at his house in Coyoacan, a fashionable suburb of Mexico City, where he lived with Helena Lupescu in 1942.

(*Left*) King Carol in a portrait widely used for propaganda purposes in Rumania during the early months of the Second World War.

(*Right*) A philatelist and his wife arrive at Dover for the International Stamp Exhibition in London in 1950. The only vestige of former glory and notoriety was that the ex-King and the Princess were afforded diplomatic privileges through the Customs.

enormous rabble howling for the King's abdication could accompany him.

He swaggered into the King's study and said without any preamble that he could only accept the office of Prime Minister, provided he had complete authority to give or withhold privileges according to the nation's will. He hinted clearly that he was ready to demand the King's abdication.

When Carol remained silent, Antonescu then produced documents which, he said, it was his duty to request the King to sign.

"They cancel the Constitution of 1938, your Majesty," he explained. The meaning was obvious. By the 1938 Constitution, Carol had taken over autocratic powers. These were now to be stripped from him.

Carol lost his temper and rose to his feet, his fist clenched and his face mottled with anger. "Your words are high treason," he warned the General.

"So far only one of the two people in this room has committed high treason, your Majesty," the General replied calmly. "That also was in time of war."

Antonescu had deliberately attacked Carol on one of the most sensitive points in his memory—the time that he had fled to Russia in order to marry Zizi.

Carol spluttered incoherently. His arm pointed to the door. Eventually he was able to mouth what he wanted to say. "Get out!" he screamed. Antonescu's mouth curled in a derisive smile. He clicked his heels, turned and walked in soldierly fashion from the room.

Hardly had he gone than Helena, who had been eavesdropping at the other door, rushed in and on her knees begged Carol to call Antonescu back. Sheepishly Carol did so.

"I am ready to sign," he said.

Immediately Antonescu's manner changed.

"That is excellent news, your Majesty," he said with great deference. "I am honoured with the faith you place

G

in my ability to keep the nation together. I shall, of course, consult members of all political parties and all the senior officers of the Army. It will naturally be necessary to give Cabinet rank to the leaders of the Iron Guard. They will, I am sure, be as anxious as I am to maintain your Majesty's position."

The two men shook hands and parted in an almost friendly fashion.

Carol was his old self at luncheon time and tried to convince Helena, who was the only person present, that all, despite her forebodings, would be well. In mid-afternoon, Antonescu returned to the palace and again conferred with the King. This time the General pressed hard on the advantages he had gained. He insinuated that the conferences he had held since the morning interview indicated that the position in the country was more dangerous than either of them had realised. He demanded, in fact, dictatorial powers.

The meeting lasted an hour, but most of the fight had gone out of Carol and Antonescu was able to leave with a Royal Decree in which the General was given full powers to rule Rumania.

Carol remained a King, but a King only in name. He still had the right to grant pardons and amnesties and it was his signature that had to appear on treaties. He could also award medals and confer orders where he wished. Beyond those formal duties his power was no longer existent.

Antonescu had ably mastered the negotiating technique of Adolf Hitler. Every move of appeasement by his adversary merely resulted in fresh demands. As soon as he had left the King with the royal decree in his hand, he started to organise trouble so that he could return and demand new concessions.

Members of the Iron Guard were ordered to stir up trouble in Bucharest and if they could not make trouble, then to walk round the Palace and fire off a few revolvers.

The patriotism of the people was to be whipped up and then they were to be told to rally outside the palace and protest against the culprit.

By 9 o'clock on the evening of September 5th, rioting was proceeding according to plan in many of the streets of Bucharest. Half an hour later, Antonescu, in the uniform of a full General, presented himself at the palace and demanded to see Carol immediately.

An enormous mob had assembled in the Royal Square. Down the Boulevard Elizabetta Iron Guardists were marching in formation singing their revolutionary song "Capitanul". The mob began to chant "Give us the King! Give us Lupescu! Don't let them get away!"

When Antonescu was admitted to Carol's study, he crossed to the window and threw it open so that the noise could be heard. He then turned to the King and said:

"Death is round the corner, Sire."

The King did not deign to reply, but motioned to Antonescu to sit down.

"What is the reason for this visit?" he asked.

"There is nothing for me to do but to request your abdication," Antonescu replied.

He then proceeded to outline all the misery that the King had brought to Rumania over the past ten years. He made no personal attack on the King's private life, but cleverly indicated that every economic and political trouble that Rumania had experienced was due entirely to the King's lack of wisdom.

The terrible indictment, basically unjust but seemingly true, with all its mass of circumstantial evidence, appalled Carol. Tired and dispirited as he was, he half believed what Antonescu was saying. Only occasionally did his old fire return and reject some of the wilder charges that were made. Carol concentrated his defence on the charge that Rumania, like so many other countries in Europe, had been destroyed by a Fifth Column.

"There are those of us, General," he said, "who consider patriotism is a simple word with only one meaning."

It was true that Antonescu had in his career been a true Rumanian, and it was only his lust for power that had influenced him to traduce his oath as an officer and as a subject of the King.

The charge of treachery went home and he stood up, saying that he considered it best to leave the King to think over matters for himself.

"I shall not leave the palace," he said; "but for the time being I think it would be reasonable if we both postponed our arguments."

As Antonescu crossed to the door, Prince Michael came in. The young man was white-faced and worried. Wordlessly he looked at the General, eager to know what was happening. Shamefacedly Antonescu apologised for not seeing the Prince before, excusing himself on the grounds that he had been so busy.

"Your Highness must not be worried; I can assure you that I am ready to sacrifice my life for Rumania," he muttered.

As he left the room, Michael turned to his father. Carol had slumped in an armchair and was shakily lighting a cigarette. Michael used the house telephone to summon Helena. She came with some sandwiches and a bottle of champagne. Carol told them what was happening and both assured him that whatever the future might hold they would remain by his side.

Carol grasped Helena's hand affectionately and gratefully, but to Michael he said that for him the path of duty might mean their separation. If that choice should come, there should be no question as to which way he must go.

Carol pretended to be optimistic and said that he was sure that if he refused to sign any deed of abdication, Antonescu would not dare to act. The loyalty of the Rumanian people to the Royal House was too well known.

At the same time he went closely into details of his private financial situation, should the worst occur. Ever practical, Helena was able to give him a precise account of what she herself had managed to put away for such an eventuality as this.

Shortly before 4 o'clock on the morning of September 6th an emissary from General Antonescu brought a letter. It was an ultimatum demanding that the King should agree to his abdication before 6 o'clock.

Helena quietly called for a trusted servant who sped noiselessly away to fetch Urdareanu and a few of their intimate friends. They gave Carol the necessary encouragement so that he signed the abdication as if he had been persuaded against his better judgment. He then went to a small ante-room, normally used by his aide-de-camp, and said that he wished to be left alone. There he wrote in his own hand his last message as King to the Rumanian people. It read:

"To my people. Times of great disturbance and anxiety are passing over my beloved country. For ten years since I assumed my place of high duty as King of my Fatherland I have striven incessantly day and night. With deep love I have worked to do all that my conscience dictated for the good of Greater Rumania. Now days of terrible hardship are overwhelming my country which is faced with the gravest dangers. Because of the great love I bear for my country in which I was born and reared I wish to prevent these dangers by passing to-day to my son, The Crown Prince Michael, whom I know you love very dearly, the heavy burden of Kingship. In making this sacrifice for the salvation of the Fatherland, I pray God that it shall not be in vain.

"In leaving my beloved son to my people I ask all Rumanians to protect him with their warmest love and loyalty, so that he may find all the support that he will need so much in the difficult task which henceforth will rest on his young shoulders.

"I pray that my country may be protected by the God of our Fathers, and He may grant her a glorious future. Long live Rumania.—Carol Rex."

When this document was handed to Antonescu there was an audible sigh of relief on both sides. Now that it was all over, General and King were able to speak as man to man.

"You need have no qualms, Sire, that there will be any insult to your person, or difficulty in arranging for your exodus from the country," Antonescu said. "We could, if you wish, get you to your yacht."

He turned to Helena Lupescu.

"In your case, Madame, I must confess that the people's attitude is not without some danger. This also applies to Urdareanu," he added, not giving the man any title and refraining from looking at him. "However, there should be no difficulty in arranging for your transport to the Cotroceni Palace, where I will personally guarantee that you will be able to remain in safety until arrangements can be made to get you out of the country either by air or by train."

Carol insisted immediately that both Helena and Urdareanu must come with him.

Prince Michael grasped Antonescu's hand and begged him to let him go with his father. His eyes were filled with tears. Antonescu looked at him with sympathy and seemed almost ready to acquiesce, partly because he had the characteristic Rumanian regard for the bonds between parents and children, and also perhaps because he saw that this was still another method of building up his own prestige.

But in his murmured words, which were said to himself more than to any of the people in that room, he revealed the true master of Rumania: "The Fuehrer has said that the young one must remain."

Helena saw the light of hope that had sprung into Carol's eyes when Michael showed that the love he bore for his father was so great. She affirmed harshly that the ex-King and she would agree to leave Rumania with Michael or they would not go at all. The Prince gratefully took a step towards her and moved her arm so that it was around his shoulders. Helena was very fond of Michael and he loved her. She understood him and had always been his good friend. Now, with a woman's intuition, she knew where his best path led.

"Don't upset yourself," she begged. "Your mother will now be able to return and live with you." She gave Antonescu a questioning glance, who nodded.

Carol made no sign that he had even heard when a moment later Antonescu donned his cap and formally spoke to the new King.

"I expect that you are in need of a little rest, Your Majesty. I will return in a couple of hours so that you may take the Oath of Allegiance to your Nation."

Carol and Helena retired to rest. Strong formations of troops were placed round the palace and round her villa. The roads in the vicinity were cleared of people. No objections were made to Carol when he rose shortly before luncheon and began busying himself with seeing what he could take away.

Altogether there were a hundred pieces of luggage—crates which included the El Greco masterpieces which his father had acquired, many of his valuable first editions, his vast stamp collection, the cases of butterflies and plants which he had accumulated in his youth, and all the portable valuables on which he could lay his hands.

A brief and formal message from General Antonescu informed the ex-King that a special train of three carriages would be awaiting him from dusk onwards in a siding of the goods yard outside the Bucharest main station.

A junior officer arrived at 10 o'clock and said that he had two army lorries and a platoon of men who would convey the Royal party and their luggage to the station. A car would be driven to the rear entrance of the Palace at 3.0 a.m. and it was General Antonescu's request that his ex-Majesty and any of the friends whom he wished to go with him should then be ready.

At 10 in the evening, Carol went through the underground tunnel to the New House where he took farewell of his son. When he got back to the Palace, Helena Lupescu was there as well as Urdareanu. . . . None of them had anything to say and they awaited the time for departure in a dimly illuminated room.

Rain began to fall heavily shortly after midnight. At half-past two precisely there was a knock on the door and a Palace servant announced that the car had arrived. It was driven at high speed through the city but by a roundabout route. When it slithered to a stop in the mud of the loading area beside the carriages, a Guard of Honour presented arms.

Carol alighted last and walked with leaden footsteps towards the second of the three coaches. He was in civilian clothes and he had turned up the collar of his overcoat. His head was sunken into his bowed shoulders, and he took no notice of the troops. As soon as he was aboard, an officer went forward to speak to the driver of the locomotive, and two minutes later the train set out on its long journey across Rumania.

It went by a devious route passing at high speed through all large towns, stopping only at wayside halts in order to take on water and to change the crew. It must be said in favour of General Antonescu that he had taken every possible precaution to ensure the safe passage of the train.

For the first part of the journey all three of the passengers slept through sheer exhaustion. When they arose, Helena and Urdareanu began bickering over the breakfast table, Urdareanu insinuating that all their troubles were due entirely to her. Carol stood this as long as he could, and then in the presence of the waiter angrily exclaimed: "Leave her alone, for God's sake. Whatever she has done or has not done, she did or failed to do only because of me."

For the rest of the day, Carol insisted on being alone, moving to the first carriage of the train, where he sat staring out of the window watching the panorama of his country pass his eyes for the last time. By the time darkness fell they were nearing the frontier with Jugoslavia. Carol's last glimpse of his Kingdom was of the vast wheat fields of the province of Banat glowing golden in the dying rays of the setting sun.

When there was nothing more to be seen and the train guards drew the blinds so that the coach lights could be put on, Helena came and sat beside him. He took her hands into his.

The train began to slow down a little as it crossed over the points of the large railway station at Timisoara. It moved through the station itself at little more than ten miles an hour. Beyond the platforms it gathered speed again—it was entering a stretch of line which passed between high embankments.

There was a crack from a rifle and a bullet crashed into the roof of the coach. More shots were fired, and Carol gripped Helena by the wrists and pushed her headlong to the far end of the coach where there was a bathtub. He heaved her bodily inside and stooping over the edge, held her down, forgetful of his own safety.

The train was rocking from side to side as the driver put on all speed to get away from the ambush. No one was hurt and no serious damage was done. Thirty minutes later the train came to a halt. Carol had left Rumanian territory and was in the safety of a Jugoslavian customs post near Kikinda.

15

1940–1941

CAROL had not been so unwise as to move into exile without obtaining the best possible assurances that he—and his two friends—would be safe from the more vicious exploits of Hitler—and also from that section of the Gestapo which specialised in the eradication of troublesome persons of note.

Antonescu had given guarantees, endorsed by the Nazi Foreign Ministry, that the Royal exile and his party would have safe conduct as far as the borders of neutral Portugal. True, the route was so carefully scheduled, and the time allowed so rigid, that the document was little more than a list of regulations to prisoners in transit.

The train meandered along branch lines so as to avoid crossing into Hungary, reached Zagreb by mid-afternoon, and passed through Trieste into Italy by the evening. There were long hold-ups in sidings while Italian troop trains and armament trains moved along the main lines, and it was not till the following morning that Carol reached the safety of neutral Switzerland.

The Swiss authorities had to handle the affair with great discretion. With the entry of Italy into the war and the occupation of virtually the whole of Europe by the Rome-Berlin Axis the country's neutrality was already in jeopardy. But with their traditional courtesy to refugees the Swiss made the Royal party welcome, and it was insinuated that, while the arrangements agreed with the German and Rumanian Governments precluded any chance of offering permanent sanctuary, the regulations about his time of stay would possibly be overlooked until Berlin or Bucharest made definite complaints.

The ex-King behaved like an automaton. He was suffering from nervous prostration and shock, and it was Helena who organised everything. She had great reserves of energy, and perhaps because she had for a long time seen the crash coming she was not so numbed by the disaster as her Royal lover.

It was she who forced Carol to eat, to take sleeping pills to get some rest, and persuaded him to cut down on his eternal smoking. Her care and devotion were ceaseless, but when she saw how little his health was improving she made tentative enquiries about obtaining a medical report on the advisability of his remaining in Switzerland for a prolonged rest cure. She was told that any such plan might bring about a demand for Carol's extradition on criminal charges based on "his corruption and defrauding of the Rumanian people".

Carol's depression was not the result of self-pity or fear. His thoughts in those days were entirely for his son. He was extremely fond of Michael, but seemed quite unable to realise that the boy was not really dependent on him. The new King was nineteen years of age, over 6 ft tall, and blessed with more than the normal amount of common sense at such an age.

Eagerly Carol scanned the Rumanian newspapers for news of Michael's activities. The propaganda machinery had been working at full blast in order to boost the national morale. But the photographs were not faked.

Michael's accession was undoubtedly popular. He had gone in uniform to the frontier to greet his mother, and when the Royal train drew into Bucharest enormous crowds were there to greet him—those in the front, as Carol noticed, wearing the green-shirted uniform of the Iron Guard.

The welcome of the people who swarmed in the streets along which Michael and Her Majesty the Queen Mother, as she was now officially titled, drove was genuine enough. The open carriage, drawn by a team of four white horses, was frequently stopped by people anxious to demonstrate their joy. During the service of thanksgiving in the Cathedral, thousands knelt in the road as they listened to the ceremonial on the public address equipment.

"It is a long time since a Rumanian King dared to go out among his people in an open carriage," was Carol's weary comment as he put the newspapers aside. "God grant that Michael may never know it otherwise."

The prayer was not answered. The enthusiasm of the mob was rapidly suppressed by the organised suspicion of the Iron Guard, whose members began their whispering campaign summarised in the comment: "Like father, like son". Within a month German formations were in the country. With their backing, Antonescu proclaimed himself Conducator of Rumania—monarch, general, chief minister all rolled into one. Michael reigned on sufferance.

On other pages of the Rumanian newspapers in those first days of Carol's exile were filthy "revelations" of the ex-King's misrule. The cession of territory was, of course, not referred to because of the Nazi contribution to this. Instead, specious arguments were printed indicating that the country's economic chaos was due entirely to the corrupt activities of the King, Urdareanu, and "the Jewess Lupescu".

Carol himself was branded as an embezzler, a swindler, and "an epileptic pervert". There was just enough basis for the charges of financial malpractice to give a tinge of veracity to the generalisations.

But the tone of the attacks which worried Carol most was the virulent campaign against Helena. It was suggested that national honour and international justice would demand her return under arrest and eventual trial.

These forebodings lifted him out of his attitude of hopeless lethargy. He started to dream of a noble renaissance of his cause as the head of a free Rumanian group. He believed that it might be possible to reach London, and there, like the Queen of the Netherlands, the King of Norway, and General de Gaulle, he could rally the democratic forces of his people and begin the long fight back.

It was characteristic of his disregard for unpleasant facts that he ignored the difficulty that Rumania was not and never had been at war with Germany; that he himself was badly tainted with Nazi practices, including anti-Semitism; and that there was hardly a Rumanian outside the borders of the country to rally to his side.

By September 12th, the Swiss authorities had to request Carol to resume his journey. Unknown to him, Bucharest Radio announced on the day when Carol's private coaches rumbled across Vichy France at the rear of a normal passenger train that the arrangements to permit the ex-King and his party to reside in Portugal had been cancelled. Authorisation would be for residence in Spain.

Of course King Michael had nothing to do with this treacherous reversal of a solemn promise. Antonescu was already not troubling to consult his monarch on such matters, and the young King was not even given the courtesy of a report on what his Government was doing. Equally in fairness, it must be said that the Conducator had not wished to forbid the ex-King to rot his life away in Portugal.

The order came from Ribbentrop on the advice of Heinrich Himmler. The Gestapo chief, with orders from Hitler to keep Carol under constant surveillance, had considerable misgivings as to the possibility of doing this in neutral Portugal. In pro-Axis Spain, however, his organisation was perfect.

The exiles' train took two days to reach the Spanish frontier. At the last town on the French side, Cerbère, south of Perpignan, Carol learned of the new arrangements for the first time. General Franco had sent three coaches which were splendidly equipped and furnished, but the deference to his Royal rank did not disguise the fact that, whatever Carol desired, the destination would be Barcelona and that the doors would be locked till the train arrived.

Actually accommodation for the party had been arranged by the Spanish Government in a hotel in the seaside resort of Sitges, twenty miles beyond Barcelona. The Spanish Secret Service kept the guests incommunicado from the press and forbade them to leave the hotel, except for exercise in the grounds. To all intents and purposes they were prisoners.

When the onset of severe winter weather made it ridiculous for the Royal exile to remain on the coast, Carol was invited to move into the Andalusia Palace Hotel at Seville. After a brief stay in Madrid he arrived there in December, 1940.

By this time a number of Rumanians and other nationals Carol and Helena had known during their days of exile in France had managed to join his retinue. Some were servants who had a genuine liking for their old master and mistress; a few were members of the "international set" which had used the French capital and the Riviera as its playground ever since the first world war. They had fled to Spain when the German break-through occurred in the early summer.

The result was that, counting servants and friends, the party which hoped to find inexpensive accommodation provided by the Spanish Government in Seville numbered forty. They were disappointed. Only two rooms had been reserved at the hotel.

The restricted accommodation presented a most delicate problem. Carol was aware that if Helena and he occupied the same bedroom, the intensely Catholic Spanish would be offended by such blatant misbehaviour. If they occupied separate rooms there would be no room for Urdareanu.

The ex-King had by this time fully recovered, and

with a return to good physical health his temper was again typically short and effective in getting things done. A room, small and austere, was found for Urdareanu. Carol's valet and Helena's maid found lodgings nearby, and those friends who considered it still worth while to remain loyal and faithful put up at various other hotels.

It must be admitted that the reasonable comfort and comparative luxury which Carol was gradually able to attain during the winter of 1940–41 was not wholly due to the impact of his personality and rank, nor to the generosity of the Spanish Government. He simply bought what he wanted.

Thanks largely to Helena's precautions he was in affluence. One suitcase among the hundred pieces of luggage that had been loaded on the train at Bucharest was crammed with banknotes in half a dozen European currencies. They had been assiduously collected over months by Helena on a personal understanding with a director of the Rumanian bank. Swiss francs and American dollars could buy almost anything Carol required.

They bought him contacts in Portugal and Gibraltar. The Portuguese border and the British fortress were within a hundred miles of Seville and he was envisaging both as potential places of refuge.

Whether the go-betweens who claimed to be able to reach the ear of the British Secret Service in Gibraltar spoke the truth or merely made up a convenient story he could not judge. In any event the result was the same. There seemed no likelihood that Great Britain would co-operate in facilitating his escape.

The Portuguese possibilities were much better. Reliable messages from members of the Rumanian diplomatic service who were known personally to Carol and whom he could trust, informed him that Lisbon's strict interpretation of complete neutrality would guarantee his safety if he could get across the border.

Carol found a new zest for life now that he could plan

and intrigue on a melodramatic scheme for getting to freedom. He was delighted, when he sent a formal application to General Franco to be permitted to pur-chase a car and to drive around the district for recreation, to have his request granted.

There were provisions that he would always have to submit his itinerary in advance, and would not complain if a police car escorted him. To this Carol made no objec-tion at all, and the pleasure drives became a daily occur-rence. At first they were of short duration, but by February, 1941, he was asking for, and obtaining, per-mission to be out all day and to drive on roundabout routes of 150 miles and more. He invariably took Helena in the seat beside him and Ernest Urdareanu at the back.

It was Helena's job to watch the following police car in the driving mirror and Urdareanu's to memorise distances and position of every road and by-road they used. By the beginning of March, Carol had an encyclo-paedic knowledge of the roads for a hundred miles to the West of Seville.

Helena had reported that the police car no longer troubled to accelerate when he drove recklessly to see what speed he could get out of the car on a mile or so of straight road; they had learned after the first few occa-sions that he always slowed down and waited for the escort to catch up.

He was ready to make his bid for freedom just in time. Friendly Spaniards warned Carol on the evening of March 2nd that a serious problem had arisen.

Hitler was exerting heavy pressure on General Franco to enter the war on the Axis side. Among the welter of threats and blandishments was a significant suggestion that the Third Reich was ready to take over the responsi-bility of accommodating Carol.

He would be treated with all the respect due to a person of Royal blood and could be assured of a life com-parable with that being enjoyed by Leopold of the

Belgians. There were several castles the Nazi government were considering as a suitable residence. It might even be possible to arrange that he lived in one that had originally been owned by his great-uncle before he ascended the Rumanian throne.

Carol was fully cognizant of Spain's position in the new Europe and realised that there was no time to be lost. Until late that night the three conspirators discussed various routes and times. They decided on a trip ostensibly to Huelva and the coastal area around the town for the purpose of picknicking in the spring sunshine. Then they would inform their guards that they intended to drive back to the west of the river on a roundabout route so as to touch the foothills of the Sierra Morena.

There was some sharp bickering about the question of luggage and treasured possessions. Carol insisted that the suitcase of money and a couple of overnight cases were all that they dared to take. Even those would be difficult to smuggle into the hotel garage and conceal in the car boot. Helena saw the sense of this, and privately reassured herself about the future by pondering on the amount of jewellery she could conceal under the heavy fur coat she proposed to wear. Urdareanu was not so amenable. His greedy mind boggled at the thought of abandoning everything.

But Carol, whose intolerance for his crony had grown steadily ever since they left Rumania, harshly told him that the choice was his: he could either come in the clothes he stood up in or remain behind to enjoy the hospitality of the Fuehrer. Urdareanu went off to bed in a sulk.

The next morning was cold, but brilliantly sunny. The proposal of a day-long tour with a midday picnic did not seem at all absurd, and Carol's route was approved by his detective-guards.

The luncheon baskets were opened on the roadside near Huelva. Carol had selected the wine with care, and there was some excellent brandy to keep the cold out. The three detectives in the escort car were delighted to drink the ex-King's health, and they admiringly listened to his boasts that during the afternoon he really intended to see what the car could do. He added that if they lost sight of him he would await them where his route joined the main road from the Spanish border to Seville.

It was said by the German news service afterwards that Carol crossed into Portugal skulking in the boot of the car, and that he was so cramped and frightened when the Portuguese customs officials opened it that he had to be laid flat in the road till he recovered.

It was quite untrue. Carol was at the wheel when the car slithered to a stop after a seventy-miles-per-hour dash to safety. The impatient party showed passports which, though false in name, were perfectly in order. The barrier was raised, and the car went on. The Spanish detectives were nowhere in sight. They had obediently gone to the rendezvous on the main Seville road. Not until some hours later did they telephone the news that their charge had eluded them.

By that time, Carol was making for Lisbon, and the "graveyard of Royalty"—Estoril.

16

CAROL'S escape to neutral Portugal was more than an escape to safety. It was a journey out of history.

Hitler's agents in Spain, after making a few protests about Spanish slackness just as a matter of principle, wrote off the ex-King's name as a risk to the New Order.

In Rumania, Carol remained a scapegoat for every trouble, past, present or prophesied. The "Jewess Lupescu" appeared sporadically in newspaper cartoons, and her name was yelled as the Iron Guard rowdies smashed up yet another Jewish shop. A few genuine patriots stored in their memories the hated name of Urdareanu, hoping that one day they might wreak vengeance on the man they considered the insidious wrecker of the Carol regime.

Great Britain, staggering under the full weight of the Nazi terror blitz, and rallying her forces to help Yugoslavia and Greece reeling under the onslaught of the Panzer divisions and the dive bombers, had neither opportunity nor inclination to bolster up an already lost cause.

Carol and his mistress began to live a futile, hopeless existence which was the pattern of their lives until death brought the only possible solution.

Carol hated Estoril. For the first time in his chequered career he appeared almost pathetically comic. The pleasant seaside resort was full of old-fashioned aristocrats and displaced royal personages, each acutely jealous of the others and ridiculously sensitive about convention and precedence even if the imagined slight came from a hotel door-man or cafe waiter.

Carol found that the pretenders to the non-existent thrones of France and Russia, the ex-archdukes and Germanic princes, the ageing dowagers and duchesses, were quite impressed with the fact that he had been a reigning King. But they were horrified that he treated his mistress with open courtesy and expected others to do her all the honours of a King's consort.

Spitefully they gossiped about his trivial misdemeanours which were more hurtful to his self-esteem than all the shrieking Nazi propaganda with its allegations of major crimes.

They gleefully recounted how he had left his bill unpaid at the hotel in Seville, how the four dogs his mistress had acquired had been destroyed because he had refused to have them in the car on the flight to freedom, how the need to economise for the future meant that he had to clean his own shoes.

Angry and frustrated, Carol started a campaign to get to the United States. His motive was not merely to find more amenable conditions in which to live. He believed that he might be able to obtain some of the considerable sums of Rumanian gold held by American banks, and in any event the securities which Helena had salted away in half a dozen South American states were valueless until they could cross the Atlantic.

Officially, the United States had no wish to receive him with or without Helena. Also, Urdareanu was definitely on the banned list. Carol enlisted the help of Elliott Roosevelt, son of the President, and of Cornelius Vanderbilt, Jnr., but they made no headway against the State Department. A public relations expert who tried next was an expensive failure.

But there was nothing to stop Carol's party from taking a cruise. They went to Madeira and thence to Bermuda, arriving in mid-May. There Carol was able to obtain some much-needed cash through negotiations with a Mexican bank, and something of the old playboy returned in his behaviour. He and Helena were seen in the most fashionable restaurants, and they attracted a good number of American companions among the type who were only too happy to be friends of a Royal personage, whether he had a throne or not.

Helena, her famous red hair thinning and greying, bought two Pekinese which she took everywhere with her. It was said that they ranked slightly in front of Ernest Urdareanu who could usually be seen walking along behind the dogs.

At the end of the month, Carol and Helena made reservations on a cruising liner starting a tour of the Caribbean. The vessel was the *America*, and the majority of her passengers had boarded her in New York.

Washington was by that time receiving persistent reports of the imminence of an attack by Germany on the Soviet Union, and the U.S. Government was preparing for every action short of war. Large forces were to be landed in Iceland, and for this and future projects it was inevitable that troop transports would be needed. Just after Carol and his mistress had gone on board, the U.S. Navy commandeered the *America* and the passengers were turned off.

The cancellation of the cruise was bitterly disappointing to Carol, for he had planned to remain on the ship when it returned to New York, confident that even if there was a formal refusal to allow him to land, matters would quickly be smoothed over rather than to cause an incident reflecting on the United States' hospitality to "war refugees".

He under-estimated the determination of the U.S. Government to keep him out. When Helena later applied for a visa for a temporary visit in order, as she stated on her application, to have her face lifted by a well-known plastic surgeon, the answer was still a categorical "no".

Mexico City was their next resting place. There the trio drank too much, quarrelled often, and upset a number of shopkeepers regarding unpaid bills. Money problems became pressing because securities were tied up in Switzerland and Spain, so all three formed a company and opened a night club. It failed when the patrons who flocked at first in the hopes of seeing an ex-King and a notorious Royal mistress had to be satisfied with the mincing Urdareanu.

The trio moved to Brazil. For most of the time they lived in Rio de Janeiro, of little importance among the large numbers of wealthy refugees from Europe. Carol was fading from the political picture through force of circumstance. A world at war had no time and no interest in an ex-King and his love affair.

He watched his unhappy country go down into the abyss of destruction as Antonescu obstinately ignored the calls of the British and United States Governments that he should redress his errors and free himself from his alliance with Hitler. He read of the rape of his kingdom as the Russians advanced to "liberate" it, while the German bombers methodically blew up the centre of Bucharest, destroying his own New House in the palace grounds and badly damaging the conference room where he had made his last stand against his pro-Nazi ministers.

There was no comfort for Carol in the news that the post-war Communist-dominated government had taken Antonescu and every associate of his before a People's Court and shot them; still less that among the 200,000 men and women in prison on political charges were his old but critical friend Maniu, various members of the Bratianu family and all court officials and highly placed army officers who had not escaped or had not voluntarily asked to be "politically re-educated".

Carol saw, more clearly than his ex-wife Helen or his son Michael, that the brief era of Rumanian monarchy was ending. The one last factor which had for all these years prevented him from taking Helena in legal marriage —that he was the proud scion of a great and illustrious Royal line and she a commoner—was no longer valid. He talked of marriage.

The "death-bed ceremony" in Rio de Janeiro on July 7th, 1947, is the most mysterious of all the inexplicable activities in the lives of these remarkable people. Without any hint that anything was wrong, it was announced simultaneously that Helena Lupescu was dying of an incurable disease and that her marriage would take place immediately by a civil ceremony.

What Helena's trouble was no one seemed to know. The very vagueness of the statement suggested the worst in the inevitable way that press reports insinuate one particular disease simply by refraining from naming it.

The story was dramatic and romantic, all of a piece in the life of Carol. But in Britain and most of the world it was not even a nine hours' wonder because of the vastly better love story which broke two days later with the announcement of the engagement of Princess Elizabeth to Lieutenant Philip Mountbatten.

A rather blurred radioed photograph of a reclining Helena with her bridegroom sitting anxiously beside her as their union was registered under Brazilian law seemed to be but a tragic preface to an obituary notice.

Perhaps a surgeon, as surgeons often are, was mistaken in his diagnosis. Perhaps Helena, then fifty years of age, was passing through one of those physiological crises in feminine middle age which are as alarming as they are temporary. Whatever the basis of the sensational news about her health, with its even more sensational gesture from her lover, time proved that all was well.

Princess Helena—as the ex-King announced his wife would henceforth be known—was able to undertake and enjoy the voyage back to Estoril and the bridal home that Carol had bought there.

The last years of Carol's life were quiet and uneventful.

Gone were all his ambitions to make a name for himself by personal achievement: gone, too, was his sensitivity about his Royal lineage, although he remained critical and hostile if anyone slighted Helena or forgot his own rather rigid standards of etiquette.

The regularisation of his union had, of course, banished every motive of his neighbours in refusing to call on Princess Helena or to accept invitations to the ex-King's home. Life, if monotonous, was pleasant.

His most intimate friend was his neighbour, the Archduke Franz Josef of Austria. It was said that Carol even contributed towards the cost of educating his two children.

The big white house overlooking the sea was named Mar y Sol (the House of the Sun). It had a magnificent garden which Carol and Helena tended themselves, with the assistance of a boy or two for the heavy work. There Helena grew her pink azaleas as she had done at her Bucharest villa, and there, in nostalgic memory of the Royal Square outside the Palace in his capital, Carol planted hundreds of gladioli.

There was a rather silly attempt to organise the household as a miniature court. The inadequate staff of servants wore shabby livery and were prone to open the door to visitors with the stains of their menial tasks in the kitchen on the tunic and breeches.

In front of the large black marble fireplace, where on wintry days Carol loved to have a "real English country house fire of logs", there was a circular table bearing a large book embossed in gold with a Crown and the intertwined initials of C and E (using Helena's original name of Elenutza).

The visitor, asked to take a seat while the servant rushed away to call the Marshal of the Court, would presently be greeted by a rather frail little old man with a grey beard. Ernest Urdareanu had improved with age. His repellent and oily politeness of the past—always carrying with it a hint of contempt or wariness—had been replaced by a rather grateful meekness that could amuse or charm.

He would open the visitor's book, present a gold pen, and invite the visitor to sign. The grandeur of the ceremony might be spoiled by Carol striding in, dressed in a sports shirt and grey flannels, a trowel in his hand, boyishly eager to have someone to talk to; or by Helena coming from the kitchen with a smear of flour on her face. She was again cooking food in the way Carol liked so much.

The couple were rarely seen apart except when Carol played golf. Helena was not keen on sport either as a spectacle or as an exercise.

They visited the cinema every week, where a group of seats was regularly reserved. Once again the pathos of his position was all too evident. If by good fortune some friends had turned up, then the party went unescorted. If, as was usual, no one wanted to accompany them, then Urdareanu came along, bringing an accountant or lawyer, or some other professional man who assisted in looking after Carol's affairs.

The ex-King liked his arrival to be marked by a small ceremony. The management of the cinema was quite ready to fall in with the idea. On receiving Urdareanu's telephone call announcing the time of the Royal party's arrival, the ordinary patrons were held back for a few minutes, a small bouquet was presented to Helena, and the house lights remained up until the visitors were seated.

Once there was a tremendous fuss because Carol did not arrive at the stated time and the screening proceeded. He was informed in so many words that the requirements of the majority had to take precedence over Royal requirements if they meant delay and disturbance.

Carol threatened to withdraw his patronage and to see that all his friends did the same, but it was noticed that ever afterwards he arrived in the foyer with the traditional punctuality of princes.

In the evenings he spent hours over his stamp collection. The hobby of his early manhood had become a valuable source of income since his exile. In the depression of the thirties he had started buying rare stamps as an investment. Helena had encouraged this during her precautionary activities to ensure a means of support should the worst happen.

During their brief stay in Switzerland in 1940 and throughout the period of the war in Spain, Portugal and Mexico, Carol had discovered that trading in stamps, easily smuggled and not easily subjected to export and import control, offered useful sources of finance.

His deep knowledge of philately, with his basic collection as the capital with which to work, made him an admired authority. The greatest dealers in London, Paris, and Zurich knew him as a hard-headed seller and an astute buyer.

His interest in stamp collecting brought him out of retirement in May, 1950, when he visited a philately exhibition at Grosvenor House, London.

Carol had what psychologists would describe as a wish-fear that the traditional embarrassing questions would be asked by hordes of journalists. Nothing of the kind occurred. The Foreign Office made no special arrangements for his arrival, regarding him as a private individual. News editors correctly assessed his publicity value as no more than that of any other minor royalty displaced by the events of the second world war.

The press photographers at the exhibition naturally concentrated on Helena and himself as the most photogenic angle on a rather dreary assignment. Carol, plumper of body and more haggard of face than on the last occasion when he attracted the lenses of the newsmen—when he celebrated his "death bed" marriage—looked younger than his fifty-seven years.

Helena was decidedly plump, and expensive corsetting could not entirely disguise the fact. Her face was rounded and heavily made up. Pencil-line eyebrows accentuated the brightness of her still magnetic and surprisingly merry eyes. Her famous red hair was by now but a legend—it was drawn tightly back under a halo hat which displayed her fine, wide forehead. It was easy to see though that, if she was no longer the peerless beauty of Jassy of the nineteen-twenties, her acumen and intelligence made her a desirable companion for an ageing man.

Rather cruelly it was said that in desperation Helena contrived to make herself news on that visit to the stamp show. On leaving she slipped on the carpeted stairs and fell heavily. . . . She lay at the foot of the staircase, moaning quietly. Carol rushed to her side and helped her up. She was taken to a private room and a doctor was summoned.

It was a genuine accident. Helena was far shorter than any of the rare photographs of her indicated—or than anyone seeing her might have guessed. She was not the sort of woman who revelled in being the modest Eve looking up in worship and adoration to her dominant Adam, and Carol was more than six feet tall. In consequence she always wore high heels, even in her boudoir. On the London visit the heels were more than three inches high, and they were the reason that she fell.

Friends who suggested to Carol that he might like to see how London night life had changed since his last visit in 1938 were told: "You forget that I'm now a grey-haired old man—and a grandfather; soon for the second time."

He said this with pride, for his affection for his son remained strong and selfless. Even if circumstances prevented any close bonds between them, he learned of all that Michael did with pleasure and satisfaction. His grand-daughter Margherita had been born in March, 1949, and a second child was expected in November.

But he was anxious not to cause any embarrassment or conflict. Carol was at this time believing implicitly that the Communist regime in Rumania would be short-lived. "One day," he used to tell everyone who asked for his opinion on political events, "Michael will swoop from the skies and regain his throne just as I did."

The visit to London was brief. Helena and he returned to their placid existence in Estoril.

After dinner on April 3rd, 1953, he complained of indigestion. It was nothing unusual. Carol had always enjoyed food and drink, and he had committed the very normal sin of people in late middle age of failing to make any adjustment in his diet as physical activity decreases. Indeed, he was consistently overeating, and his doctor had warned him that he was overweight.

This time, however, the pain became severe. Shortly before midnight, just after Helena had retired to bed, he collapsed with a heart attack. He remained conscious until the end, but was unable to speak coherently.

When Helena saw him sinking she held him in her arms.

He seemed to have had a premonition of death. Three weeks earlier he had been deeply upset with the news of the death of Zizi Lambrino in Paris. His first wife was not destitute, but very poor. Nothing was found in her bedroom which marked her brief life as a Prince's wife except her marriage certificate. Its faded and almost indecipherable Russian script proved beyond doubt that the marriage had been legal, and it was confirmed with the approval of the Odessa religious and civic authorities over a 100 Kopek stamp.

Carol shut himself away from Helena for hours after the news came through. When she felt that he should no longer brood over the past and quietly entered the room and sat beside him, he looked up and said:

"It's all ending; death brings the only news these days."

As if he intended to put his affairs in order, that evening he wrote to his legal representative in Paris and told him to negotiate the sale of his Chateau at Belleme, in the Loire valley. The place had been a useless investment he had held for more than twenty years. He had occasionally suggested to Helena that they might move there, but he never did anything about it.

Normally a hard bargainer, and ready to wait in order to get the right price in any deal, this time Carol was impatient to have things settled. All that he obtained was £7,000.

And at what was to be his last public appearance, the memorial service to Queen Mary at St. George's, Lisbon, on March 26th, he was again patently moved by the presence of death. His face was ashen white, and when he tried to utter condolences to a British diplomat his voice choked the words into incoherence.

It would not be just to say that his emotion was due to any deep affection for the Queen who had died after a life devoted to duty. He had always resented the story that when his name cropped up after the first World War, George V had branded him as "that bounder".

Even though Carol had taken tea with the Queen Mother during his 1938 visit to London he was under no illusion about her feelings towards a man who had deserted his wife for a mistress, and who, in her estimation, had dragged the cloak of Royalty into the mire of immorality and intrigue.

It was death rather than the dead that affected him so deeply on that bright spring morning.

Carol II of Greater Rumania was buried in the Royal Pantheon and Church of St. Vincent in Lisbon, where the Portuguese kings lie at rest. On the evening before his interment he lay in state in an open coffin. He was in evening dress with the cross of the Eastern Orthodox Church clasped in his hands.

Late at night, Helena, heavily veiled and in deep

mourning, entered the dimly-lit church. From the folds of her cloak she withdrew a tiny pair of scissors and cut a lock of hair from his forehead, smoothing the hair afterwards in that immaculate style which she had always known.

Her parting words were in French: "*Adieu, amour de ma vie.*"

Then she stood up and staggered backwards. Prince Andrew of Yugoslavia, Carol's nephew, who had escorted her to the church, caught her as she fainted. Carol's brother, Prince Nicolas, who had arrived to keep vigil over the body, helped to carry her outside.

The funeral ceremony next day was simple but conducted with all the deference due to a King. The wreath that lay on Carol's tomb consisted of masses of red roses tied with white ribbon. Its card bore Helena's farewell.

"To my deeply loved and unforgettable husband."

THE END

BIBLIOGRAPHY

Carol II und Madame Lupescu. Joachim von Kurenberg. 1952.
Charles I, Roi de Roumanie. Paul Lindenberg. 1913.
Contemporary Roumania. J. S. Roucer. 1932.
Helen, Queen Mother of Rumania. Arthur Gould Lee. 1956.
Histoire des Roumains. N. Jorga. 1920.
King Carol, Hitler and Lupescu. A. L. Easterman. 1942.
La Terre et La Race Roumaines. Alexandre Sturdza. 1904.
Making of Roumania, The. T. W. Riker. 1931.
On Tour with Queen Marie. Constance Lily Morris. 1927.
Plea for Rumania, A. Dimitri Dimanescu. 1941.
Roumania and Great Britain. A. Herscovici Hurst. 1919.
Roumanian Handbook, The. Norman L. Forter and Demeter B. Rostovsky. 1931.
Roumanie Nouvelle, La. Marcel Gillard. 1922.
Rumania. George Logio. 1932.
Rumania under the Soviet Yoke. Reuben Markhan. 1949.
Story of My Life, The. Marie, Queen of Rumania. 1930.
Istoria Românilor. A.D. Xenopol. 1926.
" Roumania " in the Balkans. D. Mitrany. 1915.
The Land and the Peasant in Roumania. D. Mitrany. 1930.
Politics and Political Parties in Roumania. John Clark. 1936.
A History of the Roumanians from Roman Times to the Completion of Unity. R. W. Seton-Watson. 1934.
" Roumania " in Nations of the Day. N. Jorga. 1924.
Regina Maria. N. Jorga. 1924.
Contemporary Roumania and Her Problems. J. Roucek. 1932.
United Roumania. C. U. Clark. 1932.
Roumanie. G. Alexiand and M. Antonescu. 1933.

Date Due

MAR 1 1947			

Lightning Source UK Ltd.
Milton Keynes UK
UKHW022140060223
416587UK00005B/140

9 781013 580314